# Constitutional Law

**Fifth Edition**

*2017 Supplement*

2017 Supplement

# Constitutional Law

**Fifth Edition**

**Erwin Chemerinsky**
*Dean and Professor of Law*
*University of California, Berkeley School of Law*

Published by Wolters Kluwer in New York.

Wolters Kluwer Legal & Regulatory U.S. serves customers worldwide with CCH, Aspen Publishers, and Kluwer Law International products. (www.WKLegaledu.com)

To contact Customer Service, e-mail customer.service@wolterskluwer.com, call 1-800-234-1660, fax 1-800-901-9075, or mail correspondence to:

Wolters Kluwer
Attn: Order Department
PO Box 990
Frederick, MD 21705

Printed in the United States of America.

1 2 3 4 5 6 7 8 9 0

ISBN 978-1-4548-8250-3

# About Wolters Kluwer Legal & Regulatory U.S.

Wolters Kluwer Legal & Regulatory U.S. delivers expert content and solutions in the areas of law, corporate compliance, health compliance, reimbursement, and legal education. Its practical solutions help customers successfully navigate the demands of a changing environment to drive their daily activities, enhance decision quality and inspire confident outcomes.

Serving customers worldwide, its legal and regulatory portfolio includes products under the Aspen Publishers, CCH Incorporated, Kluwer Law International, ftwilliam.com and MediRegs names. They are regarded as exceptional and trusted resources for general legal and practice-specific knowledge, compliance and risk management, dynamic workflow solutions, and expert commentary.

# Contents

# Preface

This Supplement presents the Supreme Court's decisions from October Term 2016, which ended on Monday, June 26, 2017. It was an unusual term in that there were only eight justices from the first Monday in October until the April argument calendar. There were fewer decisions than in recent years and fewer on the most controversial issues.

One of the most important developments of the term occurred on the last day when the Supreme Court granted review on two cases challenging President Trump's "travel ban." The Court also issued an opinion lifting the injunction in part and continuing the injunction in part. I have presented this as an introduction to the Supplement since professors may choose to cover it in many different ways.

Other major cases of the term presented in the Supplement are:

*Murr v. Wisconsin* — Chapter 6 — concerning the takings clause and how to determine what is the "property."

*Bethune Hill v. Virginia State Board of Elections* and *Cooper v. Harris* — Chapter 7 — concerning the use of race in drawing election district lines. Also presented is *Pena-Rodriguez v. Colorado* on race and jury deliberations.

*Pavan v. Smith* — Chapter 8 — regarding the constitutionality of denying a married same-sex couple of the ability to list both parents on a child's birth certificate.

Three free speech cases — *Matal v. Tam, Packingham v. North Carolina*, and *Expressions Hair Design v. Schneiderman* — are presented in Chapter 9.

Finally, one of the most important decisions of the term, *Trinity Lutheran, Columbia, Missouri v. Pauley*, involved whether the denial of aid to a religious institution infringed free exercise of religion. It is presented in Chapter 10.

I will continue to prepare a Supplement each summer and a new edition every four years. I welcome comments and suggestions from users of the casebook and the supplement.

Erwin Chemerinsky
Berkeley, California
July 2017

# Constitutional Law

**Fifth Edition**

*2017 Supplement*

# Introduction

On January 27, President Trump issued an Executive Order limiting travel to the United States, especially from seven countries that are comprised almost entirely of Muslims. After the United States Court of Appeals for the Ninth Circuit upheld an injunction to keep this from going into effect, President Trump issued a new Executive Order, that is now before the Supreme Court. The order suspends the entire refugee program for 120 days. It caps the total number of refugees admitted this fiscal year at 50,000 instead of 110,000. It bars immigrants from Sudan, Syria, Iran, Libya, Somalia, and Yemen for 90 days. The prior Executive Order also included Iraq, which is not on this list. Unlike the earlier Executive Order, the new version does not exclude those who have the lawful right to be in the United States, such as those with green cards and visas.

The United States Court of Appeals for the Fourth Circuit in Richmond, Virginia concluded that the travel ban could not go into effect because it was based on impermissible religious animus against Muslims. Soon after, the Ninth Circuit, which is headquartered in San Francisco, also upheld an injunction against the travel ban, saying that it likely violated federal laws that prohibit the federal government from discriminating based on nationality in its immigration decisions.

The United States government asked the Supreme Court to hear these cases and to allow the travel ban to be implemented immediately.


### TRUMP v. INTERNATIONAL REFUGEE ASSISTANCE PROJECT
137 S. Ct. ___ (2017)

PER CURIAM.

These cases involve challenges to Executive Order No. 13780, Protecting the Nation From Foreign Terrorist Entry Into the United States. The order alters practices concerning the entry of foreign nationals into the United States by, among other things, suspending entry of nationals from six designated countries for 90 days. Respondents challenged the order in two separate lawsuits. They obtained preliminary injunctions barring enforcement of several of its provisions, including the 90–day suspension of entry. The injunctions were upheld in large measure by the Courts of Appeals.

The Government filed separate petitions for certiorari, as well as applications to stay the preliminary injunctions entered by the lower courts. We grant the petitions for certiorari and grant the stay applications in part.

I

A

On January 27, 2017, President Donald J. Trump signed Executive Order No. 13769, Protecting the National from Foreign Terrorist Entry into the United States (EO-1). EO–1 addressed policies and procedures relating to the entry of foreign nationals into this country. Among other directives, the order suspended entry of foreign nationals from seven countries identified as presenting heightened terrorism risks — Iran, Iraq, Libya, Somalia, Sudan, Syria, and Yemen — for 90 days. Executive officials were instructed to review the adequacy of current practices relating to visa adjudications during this 90–day period. EO–1 also modified refugee policy, suspending the United States Refugee Admissions Program (USRAP) for 120 days and reducing the number of refugees eligible to be admitted to the United States during fiscal year 2017.

EO–1 was immediately challenged in court. Just a week after the order was issued, a Federal District Court entered a nationwide temporary restraining order enjoining enforcement of several of its key provisions. Six days later, the Court of Appeals for the Ninth Circuit denied the Government's emergency motion to stay the order pending appeal. Rather than continue to litigate EO–1, the Government announced that it would revoke the order and issue a new one.

A second order followed on March 6, 2017. EO–2 describes "conditions in six of the . . . countries" as to which EO–1 had suspended entry, stating that these conditions "demonstrate [that] nationals [of those countries] continue to present heightened risks to the security of the United States," and that "some of those who have entered the United States through our immigration system have proved to be threats to our national security."

Having identified these concerns, EO–2 sets out a series of directives patterned on those found in EO–1. Several are relevant here. First, EO–2 directs the Secretary of Homeland Security to conduct a global review to determine whether foreign governments provide adequate information about nationals applying for United States visas. EO–2 directs the Secretary to report his findings to the President within 20 days of the order's "effective date," after which time those nations identified as deficient will be given 50 days to alter their practices.

Second, EO–2 directs that entry of nationals from six of the seven countries designated in EO–1 — Iran, Libya, Somalia, Sudan, Syria, and Yemen — be "suspended for 90 days from the effective date" of the order. EO–2 explains that this pause is necessary to ensure that dangerous individuals do not enter the United States while the Executive is working to establish "adequate standards . . . to prevent infiltration by foreign terrorists"; in addition, suspending entry will "temporarily reduce investigative burdens on agencies" during the Secretary's 20–day review. A separate section provides for case-by-case waivers of the entry bar.

Third, EO–2 suspends "decisions on applications for refugee status" and "travel of refugees into the United States under the USRAP" for 120 days following its effective date. During that period, the Secretary of State is instructed to review the adequacy of USRAP application and adjudication procedures and implement whatever additional procedures are necessary "to ensure that individuals seeking admission as refugees do not pose a threat" to national security.

Fourth, citing the President's determination that "the entry of more than 50,000 refugees in fiscal year 2017 would be detrimental to the interests of the United States," EO–2 "suspend[s] any entries in excess of that number" for this fiscal year.

Finally, § 14 of EO–2 establishes the order's effective date: March 16, 2017.

B

Respondents in these cases filed separate lawsuits challenging EO–2. As relevant, they argued that the order violates the Establishment Clause of the First Amendment because it was motivated not by concerns pertaining to national security, but by animus toward Islam. They further argued that EO–2 does not comply with certain provisions in the Immigration and Nationality Act (INA).

In No. 16–1436, a Federal District Court concluded that respondents were likely to succeed on their Establishment Clause claim with respect to § 2(c) of EO–2 — the provision temporarily suspending entry from six countries — and entered a nationwide preliminary injunction barring the Government from enforcing § 2(c) against any foreign national seeking entry to the United States. The District Court in No. 16–1540 — likewise relying on the Establishment Clause — entered a broader preliminary injunction: The court enjoined nationwide enforcement of all of §§ 2 and 6.

These orders, entered before EO–2 went into effect, prevented the Government from initiating enforcement of the challenged provisions. The Government filed appeals in both cases.

The Court of Appeals for the Fourth Circuit ruled first. On May 25, over three dissenting votes, the en banc court issued a decision in *IRAP* that largely upheld the order enjoining enforcement of § 2(c). The majority determined that respondent John Doe # 1, a lawful permanent resident whose Iranian wife is seeking entry to the United States, was likely to succeed on the merits of his Establishment Clause claim. The majority concluded that the primary purpose of § 2(c) was religious, in violation of the First Amendment: A reasonable observer familiar with all the circumstances—including the predominantly Muslim character of the designated countries and statements made by President Trump during his Presidential campaign—would conclude that § 2(c) was motivated principally by a desire to exclude Muslims from the United States, not by considerations relating to national security. Having reached this conclusion, the court upheld the preliminary injunction prohibiting enforcement of § 2(c) against any foreign national seeking to enter this country.

A unanimous panel [of the Ninth Circuit] held in favor of respondents the State of Hawaii and Dr. Ismail Elshikh, an American citizen and imam whose Syrian mother-in-law is seeking entry to this country. Rather than rely on the constitutional grounds supporting the District Court's decision, the court held that portions of EO–2 likely exceeded the President's authority under the INA. On that basis it upheld the injunction as to the § 2(c) entry suspension, the § 6(a) suspension of refugee admissions, and the § 6(b) refugee cap. The Ninth Circuit, like the Fourth Circuit, concluded that the injunction should bar enforcement of these provisions across the board, because they would violate the INA "in all applications." The court did, however, narrow the injunction so that it would not bar the Government from undertaking the internal executive reviews directed by EO–2.

On June 14, evidently in response to the argument that § 2(c) was about to expire, President Trump issued a memorandum to Executive Branch officials. The memorandum declared the effective date of each enjoined provision of EO–2 to be the date on which the injunctions in these cases "are lifted or stayed with respect to that provision."


II

The Government seeks review on several issues. . . .

In addition to seeking certiorari, the Government asks the Court to stay the injunctions entered below, thereby permitting the enjoined provisions to take effect. According to the Government, it is likely to suffer irreparable harm unless a stay issues. Focusing mostly on § 2(c), and pointing to the descriptions of conditions in the six designated nations, the Government argues that a 90–day pause on entry is necessary to prevent potentially dangerous individuals from entering the United States while the Executive reviews the adequacy of information provided by foreign governments in connection with visa adjudications. Additionally, the Government asserts, the temporary bar is needed to reduce the Executive's investigative burdens while this review proceeds.

A

To begin, we grant both of the Government's petitions for certiorari and consolidate the cases for argument. The Clerk is directed to set a briefing schedule that will permit the cases to be heard during the first session of October Term 2017. (The Government has not requested that we expedite consideration of the merits to a greater extent.) In addition to the issues identified in the petitions, the parties are directed to address the following question: "Whether the challenges to § 2(c) became moot on June 14, 2017."

B

We now turn to the preliminary injunctions barring enforcement of the § 2(c) entry suspension. We grant the Government's applications to stay the injunctions, to the extent the injunctions prevent enforcement of § 2(c) with respect to foreign nationals who lack any bona fide relationship with a person or entity in the United States. We leave the injunctions entered by the lower courts in place with respect to respondents and those similarly situated, as specified in this opinion.

Crafting a preliminary injunction is an exercise of discretion and judgment, often dependent as much on the equities of a given case as the substance of the legal issues it presents. The purpose of such interim equitable relief is not to conclusively determine the rights of the parties, but to balance the equities as the litigation moves forward. In awarding a preliminary injunction a court must also "conside[r] . . . the overall public interest." In the course of doing so, a court "need not grant the total relief sought by the applicant but may mold its decree to meet the exigencies of the particular case."

Here, of course, we are not asked to grant a preliminary injunction, but to stay one. In assessing the lower courts' exercise of equitable discretion, we bring to bear an equitable judgment of our own. Before issuing a stay, "[i]t is ultimately necessary . . . to balance the equities — to explore the relative harms to applicant and respondent, as well as the interests of the public at large." This Court may, in its discretion, tailor a stay so that it operates with respect to only "some portion of the proceeding."

The courts below took account of the equities in fashioning interim relief, focusing specifically on the concrete burdens that would fall on Doe, Dr. Elshikh, and Hawaii if § 2(c) were enforced. They reasoned that § 2(c) would "directly affec[t]" Doe and Dr. Elshikh by delaying entry of their family members to the United States. The Ninth Circuit concluded that § 2(c) would harm the State by preventing students from the designated nations who had been admitted to the University of Hawaii from entering this country. These hardships, the courts reasoned, were sufficiently weighty and immediate to outweigh the Government's interest in enforcing § 2(c). Having adopted this view of the equities, the courts approved injunctions that covered not just respondents, but parties similarly situated to them — that is, people or entities in the United States who have relationships with foreign nationals abroad, and whose rights might be affected if those foreign nationals were excluded.

But the injunctions reach much further than that: They also bar enforcement of § 2(c) against foreign nationals abroad who have no connection to the United States at all. The equities relied on by the lower courts do not balance the same way in that context. Denying entry to such a foreign national does not burden any American party by reason of that party's relationship with the foreign national. And the courts below did not conclude that exclusion in such circumstances would impose any legally relevant hardship on the foreign national himself. So whatever burdens may result from enforcement of § 2(c) against a foreign national who lacks any connection to this country, they are, at a minimum, a good deal less concrete than the hardships identified by the courts below.

At the same time, the Government's interest in enforcing § 2(c), and the Executive's authority to do so, are undoubtedly at their peak when there is no tie between the foreign national and the United States. Indeed, EO–2 itself distinguishes between foreign nationals who have some connection to this country, and foreign nationals who do not, by establishing a case-by-case waiver system primarily for the benefit of individuals in the former category. The interest in preserving national security is "an urgent objective of the highest order." To prevent the Government from pursuing that objective by enforcing § 2(c) against foreign nationals unconnected to the United States would appreciably injure its interests, without alleviating obvious hardship to anyone else.

We accordingly grant the Government's stay applications in part and narrow the scope of the injunctions as to § 2(c). The injunctions remain in place only with respect to parties similarly situated to Doe, Dr. Elshikh, and Hawaii. In practical terms, this means that § 2(c) may not be enforced against foreign nationals who have a credible claim of a bona fide relationship with a person or entity in the United States. All other foreign nationals are subject to the provisions of EO–2.

The facts of these cases illustrate the sort of relationship that qualifies. For individuals, a close familial relationship is required. A foreign national who wishes to enter the United States to live with or visit a family member, like Doe's wife or Dr. Elshikh's mother-in-law, clearly has such a relationship. As for entities, the relationship must be formal, documented, and formed in the ordinary course, rather than for the purpose of evading EO–2. The students from the designated countries who have been admitted to the University of Hawaii have such a relationship with an American entity. So too would a worker who accepted an offer of employment from an American company or a lecturer invited to address an American audience. Not so someone who enters into a relationship simply to avoid § 2(c): For example, a nonprofit group devoted to immigration issues may not contact foreign nationals from the designated countries, add them to client lists, and then secure their entry by claiming injury from their exclusion.

In light of the June 12 decision of the Ninth Circuit vacating the injunction as to § 2(a), the executive review directed by that subsection may proceed promptly, if it is not already underway. EO–2 instructs the Secretary of Homeland Security to complete this review within 20 days, after which time foreign governments will be given 50 days further to bring their practices into line with the Secretary's directives. Given the Government's representations in this litigation concerning the resources required to complete the 20–day review, we fully expect that the relief we grant today will permit the Executive to conclude its internal work and provide adequate notice to foreign governments within the 90–day life of § 2(c).

C

The *Hawaii* injunction extends beyond § 2(c) to bar enforcement of the § 6(a) suspension of refugee admissions and the § 6(b) refugee cap. In our view, the equitable balance struck above applies in this context as well. An American individual or entity that has a bona fide relationship with a particular person seeking to enter the country as a refugee can legitimately claim concrete hardship if that person is excluded. As to these individuals and entities, we do not disturb the injunction. But when it comes to refugees who lack any such connection to the United States, for the reasons we have set out, the balance tips in favor of the Government's compelling need to provide for the Nation's security.

The Government's application to stay the injunction with respect to §§ 6(a) and (b) is accordingly granted in part. Section 6(a) may not be enforced against an individual seeking admission as a refugee who can credibly claim a bona fide relationship with a person or entity in the United States. Nor may § 6(b); that is, such a person may not be excluded pursuant to § 6(b), even if the 50,000–person cap has been reached or exceeded. As applied to all other individuals, the provisions may take effect.

Accordingly, the petitions for certiorari are granted, and the stay applications are granted in part.

Justice THOMAS, with whom Justice ALITO and Justice GORSUCH join, concurring in part and dissenting in part.

I agree with the Court that the preliminary injunctions entered in these cases should be stayed, although I would stay them in full. The decision whether to stay the injunctions is committed to our discretion, but our discretion must be "guided by sound legal principles," The two "most critical" factors we must consider in deciding whether to grant a stay are "(1) whether the stay applicant has made a strong showing that [it] is likely to succeed on the merits" and "(2) whether the applicant will be irreparably injured absent a stay." Where a party seeks a stay pending certiorari, as here, the applicant satisfies the first factor only if it can show both "a reasonable probability that certiorari will be granted" and "a significant possibility that the judgment below will be reversed." When we determine that those critical factors are satisfied, we must "balance the equities" by "explor[ing] the relative harms to applicant and respondent, as well as the interests of the public at large."

The Government has satisfied the standard for issuing a stay pending certiorari. We have, of course, decided to grant certiorari. And I agree with the Court's implicit conclusion that the Government has made a strong showing that it is likely to succeed on the merits—that is, that the judgments below will be reversed. The Government has also established that failure to stay the injunctions will cause irreparable harm by interfering with its "compelling need to provide for the Nation's security." Finally, weighing the Government's interest in preserving national security against the hardships caused to respondents by temporary denials of entry into the country, the balance of the equities favors the Government. I would thus grant the Government's applications for a stay in their entirety.

Reasonable minds may disagree on where the balance of equities lies as between the Government and respondents in these cases. It would have been reasonable, perhaps, for the Court to have left the injunctions in place only as to respondents themselves. But the Court takes the additional step of keeping the injunctions in place with regard to an unidentified, unnamed group of foreign nationals abroad. No class has been certified, and neither party asks for the scope of relief that the Court today provides. "[I]njunctive relief should be no more burdensome to the defendant than necessary to provide complete relief *to the plaintiffs*" in the case, because a court's role is "to provide relief" only "to claimants . . . who have suffered, or will imminently suffer, actual harm." In contrast, it is the role of the "political branches" to "shape the institutions of government in such fashion as to comply with the laws and the Constitution."

Moreover, I fear that the Court's remedy will prove unworkable. Today's compromise will burden executive officials with the task of deciding—on peril of contempt—whether individuals from the six affected nations who wish to enter the United States have a sufficient connection to a person or entity in this country. The compromise also will invite a flood of litigation until this case is finally resolved on the merits, as parties and courts struggle to determine what exactly constitutes a "bona fide relationship," who precisely has a "credible claim" to that relationship, and whether the claimed relationship was formed "simply to avoid § 2(c)" of And litigation of the factual and legal issues that are likely to arise will presumably be directed to the two District Courts whose initial orders in these cases this Court has now—unanimously—found sufficiently questionable to be stayed as to the vast majority of the people potentially affected.

# Chapter 6

## Economic Liberties

### D. The Takings Clause

### 2. Is There a Taking? (casebook p. 671)

With regard to regulatory takings, the issue often arises as to how to determine what is the "property." That is the issue in *Murr v. Wisconsin*.

#### MURR v. WISCONSIN
137 S. Ct. ___ (2017)

Justice KENNEDY delivered the opinion of the Court.

The classic example of a property taking by the government is when the property has been occupied or otherwise seized. In the case now before the Court, petitioners contend that governmental entities took their real property—an undeveloped residential lot—not by some physical occupation but instead by enacting burdensome regulations that forbid its improvement or separate sale because it is classified as substandard in size. The relevant governmental entities are the respondents.

Against the background justifications for the challenged restrictions, respondents contend there is no regulatory taking because petitioners own an adjacent lot. The regulations, in effecting a merger of the property, permit the continued residential use of the property including for a single improvement to extend over both lots. This retained right of the landowner, respondents urge, is of sufficient offsetting value that the regulation is not severe enough to be a regulatory taking. To resolve the issue whether the landowners can insist on confining the analysis just to the lot in question, without regard to their ownership of the adjacent lot, it is necessary to discuss the background principles that define regulatory takings.

I

The St. Croix River originates in northwest Wisconsin and flows approximately 170 miles until it joins the Mississippi River, forming the boundary between Minnesota and Wisconsin for much of its length. The lower portion of the river slows and widens to create a natural water area known as Lake St. Croix. Tourists and residents of the region have long extolled the picturesque grandeur of the river and surrounding area.

Under the Wild and Scenic Rivers Act, the river was designated, by 1972, for federal protection. The law required the States of Wisconsin and Minnesota to develop "a management and development program" for the river area. In compliance, Wisconsin authorized the State Department of Natural Resources to promulgate rules limiting development in order to "guarantee the protection of the wild, scenic and recreational qualities of the river for present and future generations."

Petitioners are two sisters and two brothers in the Murr family. Petitioners' parents arranged for them to receive ownership of two lots the family used for recreation along the Lower St. Croix River in the town of Troy, Wisconsin. The lots are adjacent, but the parents purchased them separately, put the title of one in the name of the family business, and later arranged for transfer of the two lots, on different dates, to petitioners. The lots, which are referred to in this litigation as Lots E and F, are described in more detail below.

For the area where petitioners' property is located, the Wisconsin rules prevent the use of lots as separate building sites unless they have at least one acre of land suitable for development. A grandfather clause relaxes this restriction for substandard lots which were "in separate ownership from abutting lands" on January 1, 1976, the effective date of the regulation. The clause permits the use of qualifying lots as separate building sites. The rules also include a merger provision, however, which provides that adjacent lots under common ownership may not be "sold or developed as separate lots" if they do not meet the size requirement. The Wisconsin rules require localities to adopt parallel provisions, so the St. Croix County zoning ordinance contains identical restrictions. The Wisconsin rules also authorize the local zoning authority to grant variances from the regulations where enforcement would create "unnecessary hardship."

B

Petitioners' parents purchased Lot F in 1960 and built a small recreational cabin on it. In 1961, they transferred title to Lot F to the family plumbing company. In 1963, they purchased neighboring Lot E, which they held in their own names.

The lots have the same topography. A steep bluff cuts through the middle of each, with level land suitable for development above the bluff and next to the water below it. The line dividing Lot E from Lot F runs from the riverfront to the far end of the property, crossing the blufftop along the way. Lot E has approximately 60 feet of river frontage, and Lot F has approximately 100 feet. Though each lot is approximately 1.25 acres in size, because of the waterline and the steep bank they each have less than one acre of land suitable for development. Even when combined, the lots' buildable land area is only 0.98 acres due to the steep terrain.

The lots remained under separate ownership, with Lot F owned by the plumbing company and Lot E owned by petitioners' parents, until transfers to petitioners. Lot F was conveyed to them in 1994, and Lot E was conveyed to them in 1995.

A decade later, petitioners became interested in moving the cabin on Lot F to a different portion of the lot and selling Lot E to fund the project. The unification of the lots under common ownership, however, had implicated the state and local rules barring their separate sale or development. Petitioners then sought variances from the St. Croix County Board of Adjustment to enable their building and improvement plan, including a variance to allow the separate sale or use of the lots. The Board denied the requests, and the state courts affirmed in relevant part. In particular, the Wisconsin Court of Appeals agreed with the Board's interpretation that the local ordinance "effectively merged" Lots E and F, so petitioners "could only sell or build on the single larger lot."

The Circuit Court of St. Croix County granted summary judgment to the State, explaining that petitioners retained "several available options for the use and enjoyment of their property." For example, they could preserve the existing cabin, relocate the cabin, or eliminate the cabin and build a new residence on Lot E, on Lot F, or across both lots. The court also found petitioners had not been deprived of all economic value of their property. Considering the valuation of the property as a single lot versus two separate lots, the court found the market value of the property was not significantly affected by the regulations because the decrease in value was less than 10 percent.

The Wisconsin Court of Appeals affirmed. . . . The Supreme Court of Wisconsin denied discretionary review.

## II

A central dynamic of the Court's regulatory takings jurisprudence is its flexibility. This has been and remains a means to reconcile two competing objectives central to regulatory takings doctrine. One is the individual's right to retain the interests and exercise the freedoms at the core of private property ownership. Property rights are necessary to preserve freedom, for property ownership empowers persons to shape and to plan their own destiny in a world where governments are always eager to do so for them. The other persisting interest is the government's well-established power to "adjus[t] rights for the public good." As Justice Holmes declared, "Government hardly could go on if to some extent values incident to property could not be diminished without paying for every such change in the general law." In adjudicating regulatory takings cases a proper balancing of these principles requires a careful inquiry informed by the specifics of the case. In all instances, the analysis must be driven "by the purpose of the Takings Clause, which is to prevent the government from 'forcing some people alone to bear public burdens which, in all fairness and justice, should be borne by the public as a whole.'"

This case presents a question that is linked to the ultimate determination whether a regulatory taking has occurred: What is the proper unit of property against which to assess the effect of the challenged governmental action? Put another way, "[b]ecause our test for regulatory taking requires us to compare the value that has been taken from the property with the value that remains in the property, one of the critical questions is determining how to define the unit of property 'whose value is to furnish the denominator of the fraction.'" As commentators have noted, the answer to this question may be outcome determinative. This Court, too, has explained that the question is important to the regulatory takings inquiry. "To the extent that any portion of property is taken, that portion is always taken in its entirety; the relevant question, however, is whether the property taken is all, or only a portion of, the parcel in question."

Defining the property at the outset, however, should not necessarily preordain the outcome in every case. In some, though not all, cases the effect of the challenged regulation must be assessed and understood by the effect on the entire property held by the owner, rather than just some part of the property that, considered just on its own, has been diminished in value. This demonstrates the contrast between regulatory takings, where the goal is usually to determine how the challenged regulation affects the property's value to the owner, and physical takings, where the impact of physical appropriation or occupation of the property will be evident.

While the Court has not set forth specific guidance on how to identify the relevant parcel for the regulatory taking inquiry, there are two concepts which the Court has indicated can be unduly narrow.

First, the Court has declined to limit the parcel in an artificial manner to the portion of property targeted by the challenged regulation. The second concept about which the Court has expressed caution is the view that property rights under the Takings Clause should be coextensive with those under state law. By the same measure, defining the parcel by reference to state law could defeat a challenge even to a state enactment that alters permitted uses of property in ways inconsistent with reasonable investment-backed expectations. For example, a State might enact a law that consolidates nonadjacent property owned by a single person or entity in different parts of the State and then imposes development limits on the aggregate set. If a court defined the parcel according to the state law requiring consolidation, this improperly would fortify the state law against a takings claim, because the court would look to the retained value in the property as a whole rather than considering whether individual holdings had lost all value.

## III

As the foregoing discussion makes clear, no single consideration can supply the exclusive test for determining the denominator. Instead, courts must consider a number of factors. These include the treatment of the land under state and local law; the physical characteristics of the land; and the prospective value of the regulated land. The endeavor should determine whether reasonable expectations about property ownership would lead a landowner to anticipate that his holdings would be treated as one parcel, or, instead, as separate tracts. The inquiry is objective, and the reasonable expectations at issue derive from background customs and the whole of our legal tradition.

First, courts should give substantial weight to the treatment of the land, in particular how it is bounded or divided, under state and local law. The reasonable expectations of an acquirer of land must acknowledge legitimate restrictions affecting his or her subsequent use and dispensation of the property.

Second, courts must look to the physical characteristics of the landowner's property. These include the physical relationship of any distinguishable tracts, the parcel's topography, and the surrounding human and ecological environment. In particular, it may be relevant that the property is located in an area that is subject to, or likely to become subject to, environmental or other regulation.

Third, courts should assess the value of the property under the challenged regulation, with special attention to the effect of burdened land on the value of other holdings. Though a use restriction may decrease the market value of the property, the effect may be tempered if the regulated land adds value to the remaining property, such as by increasing privacy, expanding recreational space, or preserving surrounding natural beauty. A law that limits use of a landowner's small lot in one part of the city by reason of the landowner's nonadjacent holdings elsewhere may decrease the market value of the small lot in an unmitigated fashion. The absence of a special relationship between the holdings may counsel against consideration of all the holdings as a single parcel, making the restrictive law susceptible to a takings challenge. On the other hand, if the landowner's other property is adjacent to the small lot, the market value of the properties may well increase if their combination enables the expansion of a structure, or if development restraints for one part of the parcel protect the unobstructed skyline views of another part. That, in turn, may counsel in favor of treatment as a single parcel and may reveal the weakness of a regulatory takings challenge to the law.

State and federal courts have considerable experience in adjudicating regulatory takings claims that depart from these examples in various ways. The Court anticipates that in applying the test above they will continue to exercise care in this complex area.

## IV

Under the appropriate multifactor standard, it follows that for purposes of determining whether a regulatory taking has occurred here, petitioners' property should be evaluated as a single parcel consisting of Lots E and F together.

First, the treatment of the property under state and local law indicates petitioners' property should be treated as one when considering the effects of the restrictions. As the Wisconsin courts held, the state and local regulations merged Lots E and F. The decision to adopt the merger provision at issue here was for a specific and legitimate purpose, consistent with the widespread understanding that lot lines are not dominant or controlling in every case. Petitioners' land was subject to this regulatory burden, moreover, only because of voluntary conduct in bringing the lots under common ownership after the regulations were enacted. As a result, the valid merger of the lots under state law informs the reasonable expectation they will be treated as a single property.

Second, the physical characteristics of the property support its treatment as a unified parcel. The lots are contiguous along their longest edge. Their rough terrain and narrow shape make it reasonable to expect their range of potential uses might be limited. The land's location along the river is also significant. Petitioners could have anticipated public regulation might affect their enjoyment of their property, as the Lower St. Croix was a regulated area under federal, state, and local law long before petitioners possessed the land.

Third, the prospective value that Lot E brings to Lot F supports considering the two as one parcel for purposes of determining if there is a regulatory taking. Petitioners are prohibited from selling Lots E and F separately or from building separate residential structures on each. Yet this restriction is mitigated by the benefits of using the property as an integrated whole, allowing increased privacy and recreational space, plus the optimal location of any improvements.

The special relationship of the lots is further shown by their combined valuation. Were Lot E separately saleable but still subject to the development restriction, petitioners' appraiser would value the property at only $40,000. We express no opinion on the validity of this figure. We also note the number is not particularly helpful for understanding petitioners' retained value in the properties because Lot E, under the regulations, cannot be sold without Lot F. The point that is useful for these purposes is that the combined lots are valued at $698,300, which is far greater than the summed value of the separate regulated lots (Lot F with its cabin at $373,000, according to respondents' appraiser, and Lot E as an undevelopable plot at $40,000, according to petitioners' appraiser). The value added by the lots' combination shows their complementarity and supports their treatment as one parcel.

Considering petitioners' property as a whole, the state court was correct to conclude that petitioners cannot establish a compensable taking in these circumstances. Petitioners have not suffered a taking under *Lucas,* as they have not been deprived of all economically beneficial use of their property. They can use the property for residential purposes, including an enhanced, larger residential improvement. The property has not lost all economic value, as its value has decreased by less than 10 percent.

Petitioners furthermore have not suffered a taking under the more general test of *Penn Central.* The expert appraisal relied upon by the state courts refutes any claim that the economic impact of the regulation is severe. Petitioners cannot claim that they reasonably expected to sell or develop their lots separately given the regulations which predated their acquisition of both lots. Finally, the governmental action was a reasonable land-use regulation, enacted as part of a coordinated federal, state, and local effort to preserve the river and surrounding land.

Like the ultimate question whether a regulation has gone too far, the question of the proper parcel in regulatory takings cases cannot be solved by any simple test. Courts must instead define the parcel in a manner that reflects reasonable expectations about the property. Courts must strive for consistency with the central purpose of the Takings Clause: to "bar Government from forcing some people alone to bear public burdens which, in all fairness and justice, should be borne by the public as a whole." Treating the lot in question as a single parcel is legitimate for purposes of this takings inquiry, and this supports the conclusion that no regulatory taking occurred here.

Chief Justice ROBERTS, with whom Justice THOMAS and Justice ALITO join, dissenting.

Where the majority goes astray is in concluding that the definition of the "private property" at issue in a case such as this turns on an elaborate test looking not only to state and local law, but also to (1) "the physical characteristics of the land," (2) "the prospective value of the regulated land," (3) the "reasonable expectations" of the owner, and (4) "background customs and the whole of our legal tradition." Our decisions have, time and again, declared that the Takings Clause protects private property rights as state law creates and defines them. By securing such *established* property rights, the Takings Clause protects individuals from being forced to bear the full weight of actions that should be borne by the public at large. The majority's new, malleable definition of "private property"—adopted solely "for purposes of th[e] takings inquiry," undermines that protection.

I would stick with our traditional approach: State law defines the boundaries of distinct parcels of land, and those boundaries should determine the "private property" at issue in regulatory takings cases. Whether a regulation effects a taking of that property is a separate question, one in which common ownership of adjacent property may be taken into account. Because the majority departs from these settled principles, I respectfully dissent.

Because a regulation amounts to a taking if it completely destroys a property's productive use, there is an incentive for owners to define the relevant "private property" narrowly. This incentive threatens the careful balance between property rights and government authority that our regulatory takings doctrine strikes: Put in terms of the familiar "bundle" analogy, each "strand" in the bundle of rights that comes along with owning real property is a distinct property interest. If owners could define the relevant "private property" at issue as the specific "strand" that the challenged regulation affects, they could convert nearly all regulations into *per se* takings.

And so we do not allow it. In *Penn Central Transportation Co. v. New York City,* we held that property owners may not "establish a 'taking' simply by showing that they have been denied the ability to exploit a property interest." In that case, the owner of Grand Central Terminal in New York City argued that a restriction on the owner's ability to add an office building atop the station amounted to a taking of its air rights. We rejected that narrow definition of the "property" at issue, concluding that the correct unit of analysis was the owner's "rights in the parcel as a whole." "[W]here an owner possesses a full 'bundle' of property rights, the destruction of one strand of the bundle is not a taking, because the aggregate must be viewed in its entirety."

The question presented in today's case concerns the "parcel as a whole" language from *Penn Central.* This enigmatic phrase has created confusion about how to identify the relevant property in a regulatory takings case when the claimant owns more than one plot of land. Should the impact of the regulation be evaluated with respect to each individual plot, or with respect to adjacent plots grouped together as one unit? According to the majority, a court should answer this question by considering a number of facts about the land and the regulation at issue. The end result turns on whether those factors "would lead a landowner to anticipate that his holdings would be treated as one parcel, or, instead, as separate tracts."

I think the answer is far more straightforward: State laws define the boundaries of distinct units of land, and those boundaries should, in all but the most exceptional circumstances, determine the parcel at issue. Even in regulatory takings cases, the first step of the Takings Clause analysis is still to identify the relevant "private property." States create property rights with respect to particular "things." And in the context of real property, those "things" are horizontally bounded plots of land. States may define those plots differently—some using metes and bounds, others using government surveys, recorded plats, or subdivision maps. But the definition of property draws the basic line between, as P.G. Wodehouse would put it, *meum* and *tuum.* The question of who owns what is pretty important: The rules must provide a readily ascertainable definition of the land to which a particular bundle of rights attaches that does not vary depending upon the purpose at issue.

Following state property lines is also entirely consistent with *Penn Central.* Requiring consideration of the "parcel as a whole" is a response to the risk that owners will strategically pluck one strand from their bundle of property rights—such as the air rights at issue in *Penn Central*—and claim a complete taking based on that strand alone. That risk of strategic unbundling is not present when a legally distinct parcel is the basis of the regulatory takings claim. State law defines all of the interests that come along with owning a particular parcel, and both property owners and the government must take those rights as they find them.

The majority envisions that relying on state law will create other opportunities for "gamesmanship" by landowners and States: The former, it contends, "might seek to alter [lot] lines in anticipation of regulation," while the latter might pass a law that "consolidates . . . property" to avoid a successful takings claim. But such obvious attempts to alter the legal landscape in anticipation of a lawsuit are unlikely and not particularly difficult to detect and disarm. We rejected the strategic splitting of property rights in *Penn Central*, and courts could do the same if faced with an attempt to create a takings-specific definition of "private property."

Once the relevant property is identified, the real work begins. To decide whether the regulation at issue amounts to a "taking," courts should focus on the effect of the regulation on the "private property" at issue. Adjacent land under common ownership may be relevant to that inquiry. The owner's possession of such a nearby lot could, for instance, shed light on how the owner reasonably expected to use the parcel at issue before the regulation. If the court concludes that the government's action amounts to a taking, principles of "just compensation" may also allow the owner to recover damages "with regard to a separate parcel" that is contiguous and used in conjunction with the parcel at issue.

In sum, the "parcel as a whole" requirement prevents a property owner from identifying a single "strand" in his bundle of property rights and claiming that interest has been taken. Allowing that strategic approach to defining "private property" would undermine the balance struck by our regulatory takings cases. Instead, state law creates distinct parcels of land and defines the rights that come along with owning those parcels. Those established bundles of rights should define the "private property" in regulatory takings cases. While ownership of contiguous properties may bear on whether a person's plot has been "taken," *Penn Central* provides no basis for disregarding state property lines when identifying the "parcel as a whole."


II

The lesson that the majority draws from *Penn Central* is that defining "the proper parcel in regulatory takings cases cannot be solved by any simple test." Following through on that stand against simplicity, the majority lists a complex set of factors theoretically designed to reveal whether a hypothetical landowner might expect that his property "would be treated as one parcel, or, instead, as separate tracts." Those factors, says the majority, show that Lots E and F of the Murrs' property constitute a single parcel and that the local ordinance requiring the Murrs to develop and sell those lots as a pair does not constitute a taking.

In deciding that Lots E and F are a single parcel, the majority focuses on the importance of the ordinance at issue and the extent to which the Murrs may have been especially surprised, or unduly harmed, by the application of that ordinance to their property. But these issues should be considered when deciding if a regulation constitutes a "taking." Cramming them into the definition of "private property" undermines the effectiveness of the Takings Clause as a check on the government's power to shift the cost of public life onto private individuals.

In departing from state property principles, the majority authorizes governments to do precisely what we rejected in *Penn Central* : create a litigation-specific definition of "property" designed for a claim under the Takings Clause. Whenever possible, governments in regulatory takings cases will ask courts to aggregate legally distinct properties into one "parcel," solely for purposes of resisting a particular claim. And under the majority's test, identifying the "parcel as a whole" in such cases will turn on the reasonableness of the regulation as applied to the claimant. The result is that the government's regulatory interests will come into play not once, but twice — first when identifying the relevant parcel, and again when determining whether the regulation has placed too great a public burden on that property.

Regulatory takings, however — by their very nature — pit the common good against the interests of a few. There is an inherent imbalance in that clash of interests. The widespread benefits of a regulation will often appear far weightier than the isolated losses suffered by individuals. And looking at the bigger picture, the overall societal good of an economic system grounded on private property will appear abstract when cast against a concrete regulatory problem. In the face of this imbalance, the Takings Clause "prevents the public from loading upon one individual more than his just share of the burdens of government," by considering the effect of a regulation on specific property rights as they are established at state law. But the majority's approach undermines that protection, defining property only after engaging in an ad hoc, case-specific consideration of individual and community interests. The result is that the government's goals shape the playing field before the contest over whether the challenged regulation goes "too far" even gets underway.

Put simply, today's decision knocks the definition of "private property" loose from its foundation on stable state law rules and throws it into the maelstrom of multiple factors that come into play at the second step of the takings analysis. The result: The majority's new framework compromises the Takings Clause as a barrier between individuals and the press of the public interest.

III

As I see it, the Wisconsin Court of Appeals was wrong to apply a takings-specific definition of the property at issue. Instead, the court should have asked whether, under general state law principles, Lots E and F are legally distinct parcels of land. I would therefore vacate the judgment below and remand for the court to identify the relevant property using ordinary principles of Wisconsin property law.

# Chapter 7

# Equal Protection

## C. Classifications Based on Race and National Origin

## 3. Proving the Existence of a Race or National Origin Classification

### a. Race and National Origin Classifications on the Face of the Law (casebook p. 761)

In *Pena-Rodriguez v. Colorado*, the Court considered how a court should respond to information that a juror made racist statements during jury deliberations.

### PENA-RODRIGUEZ v. COLORADO
137 S. Ct. 788 (2017)

Justice KENNEDY delivered the opinion of the Court.

The jury is a central foundation of our justice system and our democracy. Whatever its imperfections in a particular case, the jury is a necessary check on governmental power. The jury, over the centuries, has been an inspired, trusted, and effective instrument for resolving factual disputes and determining ultimate questions of guilt or innocence in criminal cases. Over the long course its judgments find acceptance in the community, an acceptance essential to respect for the rule of law. The jury is a tangible implementation of the principle that the law comes from the people.

In the era of our Nation's founding, the right to a jury trial already had existed and evolved for centuries, through and alongside the common law. The jury was considered a fundamental safeguard of individual liberty. The right to a jury trial in criminal cases was part of the Constitution as first drawn, and it was restated in the Sixth Amendment. By operation of the Fourteenth Amendment, it is applicable to the States.

Like all human institutions, the jury system has its flaws, yet experience shows that fair and impartial verdicts can be reached if the jury follows the court's instructions and undertakes deliberations that are honest, candid, robust, and based on common sense. A general rule has evolved to give substantial protection to verdict finality and to assure jurors that, once their verdict has been entered, it will not later be called into question based on the comments or conclusions they expressed during deliberations. This principle, itself centuries old, is often referred to as the no-impeachment rule. The instant case presents the question whether there is an exception to the no-impeachment rule when, after the jury is discharged, a juror comes forward with compelling evidence that another juror made clear and explicit statements indicating that racial animus was a significant motivating factor in his or her vote to convict.

## I

State prosecutors in Colorado brought criminal charges against petitioner, Miguel Angel Peña–Rodriguez, based on the following allegations. In 2007, in the bathroom of a Colorado horse-racing facility, a man sexually assaulted two teenage sisters. The girls told their father and identified the man as an employee of the racetrack. The police located and arrested petitioner. Each girl separately identified petitioner as the man who had assaulted her.

The State charged petitioner with harassment, unlawful sexual contact, and attempted sexual assault on a child. Before the jury was empaneled, members of the venire were repeatedly asked whether they believed that they could be fair and impartial in the case. A written questionnaire asked if there was "anything about you that you feel would make it difficult for you to be a fair juror." The court repeated the question to the panel of prospective jurors and encouraged jurors to speak in private with the court if they had any concerns about their impartiality. Defense counsel likewise asked whether anyone felt that "this is simply not a good case" for them to be a fair juror. None of the empaneled jurors expressed any reservations based on racial or any other bias. And none asked to speak with the trial judge.

After a 3–day trial, the jury found petitioner guilty of unlawful sexual contact and harassment, but it failed to reach a verdict on the attempted sexual assault charge. Following the discharge of the jury, petitioner's counsel entered the jury room to discuss the trial with the jurors. As the room was emptying, two jurors remained to speak with counsel in private. They stated that, during deliberations, another juror had expressed anti-Hispanic bias toward petitioner and petitioner's alibi witness. Petitioner's counsel reported this to the court and, with the court's supervision, obtained sworn affidavits from the two jurors.

The affidavits by the two jurors described a number of biased statements made by another juror, identified as Juror H.C. According to the two jurors, H.C. told the other jurors that he "believed the defendant was guilty because, in [H.C.'s] experience as an ex-law enforcement officer, Mexican men had a bravado that caused them to believe they could do whatever they wanted with women." The jurors reported that H.C. stated his belief that Mexican men are physically controlling of women because of their sense of entitlement, and further stated, " 'I think he did it because he's Mexican and Mexican men take whatever they want.' " According to the jurors, H.C. further explained that, in his experience, "nine times out of ten Mexican men were guilty of being aggressive toward women and young girls." Finally, the jurors recounted that Juror H.C. said that he did not find petitioner's alibi witness credible because, among other things, the witness was " 'an illegal.' "

After reviewing the affidavits, the trial court acknowledged H.C.'s apparent bias. But the court denied petitioner's motion for a new trial, noting that "[t]he actual deliberations that occur among the jurors are protected from inquiry under [Colorado Rule of Evidence] 606(b)." Like its federal counterpart, Colorado's Rule 606(b) generally prohibits a juror from testifying as to any statement made during deliberations in a proceeding inquiring into the validity of the verdict. The Colorado Rule reads as follows:

> "(b) Inquiry into validity of verdict or indictment. Upon an inquiry into the validity of a verdict or indictment, a juror may not testify as to any matter or statement occurring during the course of the jury's deliberations or to the effect of anything upon his or any other juror's mind or emotions as influencing him to assent to or dissent from the verdict or indictment or concerning his mental processes in connection therewith. But a juror may testify about (1) whether extraneous prejudicial information was improperly brought to the jurors' attention, (2) whether any outside influence was improperly brought to bear upon any juror, or (3) whether there was a mistake in entering the verdict onto the verdict form. A juror's affidavit or evidence of any statement by the juror may not be received on a matter about which the juror would be precluded from testifying."

The verdict deemed final, petitioner was sentenced to two years' probation and was required to register as a sex offender. . . .

Juror H.C.'s bias was based on petitioner's Hispanic identity, which the Court in prior cases has referred to as ethnicity, and that may be an instructive term here. Petitioner and respondent both refer to race, or to race and ethnicity, in this more expansive sense in their briefs to the Court. This opinion refers to the nature of the bias as racial in keeping with the primary terminology employed by the parties and used in our precedents.

## II

At common law jurors were forbidden to impeach their verdict, either by affidavit or live testimony. This rule originated in *Vaise v. Delaval* (K.B. 1785). There, Lord Mansfield excluded juror testimony that the jury had decided the case through a game of chance. The Mansfield rule, as it came to be known, prohibited jurors, after the verdict was entered, from testifying either about their subjective mental processes or about objective events that occurred during deliberations.

American courts adopted the Mansfield rule as a matter of common law, though not in every detail. The common-law development of the no-impeachment rule reached a milestone in 1975, when Congress adopted the Federal Rules of Evidence, including Rule 606(b). Congress, endorsed a broad no-impeachment rule, with only limited exceptions. The version of the rule that Congress adopted was "no accident." This version of the no-impeachment rule has substantial merit. It promotes full and vigorous discussion by providing jurors with considerable assurance that after being discharged they will not be summoned to recount their deliberations, and they will not otherwise be harassed or annoyed by litigants seeking to challenge the verdict. The rule gives stability and finality to verdicts.

Some version of the no-impeachment rule is followed in every State and the District of Columbia. Variations make classification imprecise, but, as a general matter, it appears that 42 jurisdictions follow the Federal Rule.

## III

It must become the heritage of our Nation to rise above racial classifications that are so inconsistent with our commitment to the equal dignity of all persons. This imperative to purge racial prejudice from the administration of justice was given new force and direction by the ratification of the Civil War Amendments.

"[T]he central purpose of the Fourteenth Amendment was to eliminate racial discrimination emanating from official sources in the States." In the years before and after the ratification of the Fourteenth Amendment, it became clear that racial discrimination in the jury system posed a particular threat both to the promise of the Amendment and to the integrity of the jury trial. "Almost immediately after the Civil War, the South began a practice that would continue for many decades: All-white juries punished black defendants particularly harshly, while simultaneously refusing to punish violence by whites, including Ku Klux Klan members, against blacks and Republicans." To take one example, just in the years 1865 and 1866, all-white juries in Texas decided a total of 500 prosecutions of white defendants charged with killing African–Americans. All 500 were acquitted. The stark and unapologetic nature of race-motivated outcomes challenged the American belief that "the jury was a bulwark of liberty," and prompted Congress to pass legislation to integrate the jury system and to bar persons from eligibility for jury service if they had conspired to deny the civil rights of African–Americans. Members of Congress stressed that the legislation was necessary to preserve the right to a fair trial and to guarantee the equal protection of the laws.

The duty to confront racial animus in the justice system is not the legislature's alone. Time and again, this Court has been called upon to enforce the Constitution's guarantee against state-sponsored racial discrimination in the jury system. Beginning in 1880, the Court interpreted the Fourteenth Amendment to prohibit the exclusion of jurors on the basis of race. The Court has repeatedly struck down laws and practices that systematically exclude racial minorities from juries. To guard against discrimination in jury selection, the Court has ruled that no litigant may exclude a prospective juror on the basis of race. In an effort to ensure that individuals who sit on juries are free of racial bias, the Court has held that the Constitution at times demands that defendants be permitted to ask questions about racial bias during *voir dire*.

The unmistakable principle underlying these precedents is that discrimination on the basis of race, "odious in all aspects, is especially pernicious in the administration of justice." The jury is to be "a criminal defendant's fundamental 'protection of life and liberty against race or color prejudice.'" Permitting racial prejudice in the jury system damages "both the fact and the perception" of the jury's role as "a vital check against the wrongful exercise of power by the State."


IV

This case lies at the intersection of the Court's decisions endorsing the no-impeachment rule and its decisions seeking to eliminate racial bias in the jury system. The two lines of precedent, however, need not conflict.

[R]acial bias, a familiar and recurring evil that, if left unaddressed, would risk systemic injury to the administration of justice. This Court's decisions demonstrate that racial bias implicates unique historical, constitutional, and institutional concerns. An effort to address the most grave and serious statements of racial bias is not an effort to perfect the jury but to ensure that our legal system remains capable of coming ever closer to the promise of equal treatment under the law that is so central to a functioning democracy.

Racial bias is distinct in a pragmatic sense as well. In past cases this Court has relied on other safeguards to protect the right to an impartial jury. Some of those safeguards, to be sure, can disclose racial bias. *Voir dire* at the outset of trial, observation of juror demeanor and conduct during trial, juror reports before the verdict, and nonjuror evidence after trial are important mechanisms for discovering bias. Yet their operation may be compromised, or they may prove insufficient. For instance, this Court has noted the dilemma faced by trial court judges and counsel in deciding whether to explore potential racial bias at *voir dire*. Generic questions about juror impartiality may not expose specific attitudes or biases that can poison jury deliberations. Yet more pointed questions "could well exacerbate whatever prejudice might exist without substantially aiding in exposing it."

The stigma that attends racial bias may make it difficult for a juror to report inappropriate statements during the course of juror deliberations. It is one thing to accuse a fellow juror of having a personal experience that improperly influences her consideration of the case. It is quite another to call her a bigot.

For the reasons explained above, the Court now holds that where a juror makes a clear statement that indicates he or she relied on racial stereotypes or animus to convict a criminal defendant, the Sixth Amendment requires that the no-impeachment rule give way in order to permit the trial court to consider the evidence of the juror's statement and any resulting denial of the jury trial guarantee.

Not every offhand comment indicating racial bias or hostility will justify setting aside the no-impeachment bar to allow further judicial inquiry. For the inquiry to proceed, there must be a showing that one or more jurors made statements exhibiting overt racial bias that cast serious doubt on the fairness and impartiality of the jury's deliberations and resulting verdict. To qualify, the statement must tend to show that racial animus was a significant motivating factor in the juror's vote to convict. Whether that threshold showing has been satisfied is a matter committed to the substantial discretion of the trial court in light of all the circumstances, including the content and timing of the alleged statements and the reliability of the proffered evidence.

The practical mechanics of acquiring and presenting such evidence will no doubt be shaped and guided by state rules of professional ethics and local court rules, both of which often limit counsel's post-trial contact with jurors. These limits seek to provide jurors some protection when they return to their daily affairs after the verdict has been entered. But while a juror can always tell counsel they do not wish to discuss the case, jurors in some instances may come forward of their own accord.

That is what happened here. In this case the alleged statements by a juror were egregious and unmistakable in their reliance on racial bias. Not only did juror H.C. deploy a dangerous racial stereotype to conclude petitioner was guilty and his alibi witness should not be believed, but he also encouraged other jurors to join him in convicting on that basis.

Petitioner's counsel did not seek out the two jurors' allegations of racial bias. Pursuant to Colorado's mandatory jury instruction, the trial court had set limits on juror contact and encouraged jurors to inform the court if anyone harassed them about their role in the case. Similar limits on juror contact can be found in other jurisdictions that recognize a racial-bias exception.

While the trial court concluded that Colorado's Rule 606(b) did not permit it even to consider the resulting affidavits, the Court's holding today removes that bar. When jurors disclose an instance of racial bias as serious as the one involved in this case, the law must not wholly disregard its occurrence.

The Court relies on the experiences of the 17 jurisdictions that have recognized a racial-bias exception to the no-impeachment rule—some for over half a century—with no signs of an increase in juror harassment or a loss of juror willingness to engage in searching and candid deliberations. The experience of these jurisdictions, and the experience of the courts going forward, will inform the proper exercise of trial judge discretion in these and related matters. This case does not ask, and the Court need not address, what procedures a trial court must follow when confronted with a motion for a new trial based on juror testimony of racial bias. The Court also does not decide the appropriate standard for determining when evidence of racial bias is sufficient to require that the verdict be set aside and a new trial be granted.

The Nation must continue to make strides to overcome race-based discrimination. The progress that has already been made underlies the Court's insistence that blatant racial prejudice is antithetical to the functioning of the jury system and must be confronted in egregious cases like this one despite the general bar of the no-impeachment rule. It is the mark of a maturing legal system that it seeks to understand and to implement the lessons of history. The Court now seeks to strengthen the broader principle that society can and must move forward by achieving the thoughtful, rational dialogue at the foundation of both the jury system and the free society that sustains our Constitution.

Justice THOMAS, dissenting.

The Court today holds that the Sixth Amendment requires the States to provide a criminal defendant the opportunity to impeach a jury's guilty verdict with juror testimony about a juror's alleged racial bias, notwithstanding a state procedural rule forbidding such testimony. I agree with Justice Alito that the Court's decision is incompatible with the text of the Amendment it purports to interpret and with our precedents. I write separately to explain that the Court's holding also cannot be squared with the original understanding of the Sixth or Fourteenth Amendments.

The Sixth Amendment's protection of the right, "[i]n all criminal prosecutions," to a "trial, by an impartial jury," is limited to the protections that existed at common law when the Amendment was ratified. The Sixth Amendment's specific guarantee of impartiality incorporates the common-law understanding of that term. The common law required a juror to have "freedome of mind" and to be "indifferent as hee stands unsworne." 1 E. Coke, First Part of the Institutes of the Laws of England § 234, p. 155a (16th ed. 1809).

The common-law right to a jury trial did not, however, guarantee a defendant the right to impeach a jury verdict with juror testimony about juror misconduct, including "a principal species of [juror] misbehaviour"—"notorious partiality." 3 Blackstone 388. Although partiality was a ground for setting aside a jury verdict, the English common-law rule at the time the Sixth Amendment was ratified did not allow jurors to supply evidence of that misconduct.

Perhaps good reasons exist to curtail or abandon the no-impeachment rule. Some States have done so, and others have not. Ultimately, that question is not for us to decide. It should be left to the political process described by Justice Alito. In its attempt to stimulate a "thoughtful, rational dialogue" on race relations, the Court today ends the political process and imposes a uniform, national rule. The Constitution does not require such a rule. Neither should we.

Justice ALITO with whom THE CHIEF JUSTICE and Justice THOMAS join, dissenting.

Our legal system has many rules that restrict the admission of evidence of statements made under circumstances in which confidentiality is thought to be essential. Statements made to an attorney in obtaining legal advice, statements to a treating physician, and statements made to a spouse or member of the clergy are familiar examples. Even if a criminal defendant whose constitutional rights are at stake has a critical need to obtain and introduce evidence of such statements, long-established rules stand in the way. The goal of avoiding interference with confidential communications of great value has long been thought to justify the loss of important evidence and the effect on our justice system that this loss entails.

The present case concerns a rule like those just mentioned, namely, the age-old rule against attempting to overturn or "impeach" a jury's verdict by offering statements made by jurors during the course of deliberations. For centuries, it has been the judgment of experienced judges, trial attorneys, scholars, and lawmakers that allowing jurors to testify after a trial about what took place in the jury room would undermine the system of trial by jury that is integral to our legal system.

Juries occupy a unique place in our justice system. The other participants in a trial — the presiding judge, the attorneys, the witnesses — function in an arena governed by strict rules of law. Their every word is recorded and may be closely scrutinized for missteps.

When jurors retire to deliberate, however, they enter a space that is not regulated in the same way. Jurors are ordinary people. They are expected to speak, debate, argue, and make decisions the way ordinary people do in their daily lives. Our Constitution places great value on this way of thinking, speaking, and deciding. The jury trial right protects parties in court cases from being judged by a special class of trained professionals who do not speak the language of ordinary people and may not understand or appreciate the way ordinary people live their lives. To protect that right, the door to the jury room has been locked, and the confidentiality of jury deliberations has been closely guarded.

Today, with the admirable intention of providing justice for one criminal defendant, the Court not only pries open the door; it rules that respecting the privacy of the jury room, as our legal system has done for centuries, violates the Constitution. This is a startling development, and although the Court tries to limit the degree of intrusion, it is doubtful that there are principled grounds for preventing the expansion of today's holding.

The Court justifies its decision on the ground that the nature of the confidential communication at issue in this particular case — a clear expression of what the Court terms racial bias[1] — is uniquely harmful to our criminal justice system. And the Court is surely correct that even a tincture of racial bias can inflict great damage on that system, which is dependent on the public's trust. But until today, the argument that the Court now finds convincing has not been thought to be sufficient to overcome confidentiality rules like the one at issue here.

Suppose that a prosecution witness gives devastating but false testimony against a defendant, and suppose that the witness's motivation is racial bias. Suppose that the witness admits this to his attorney, his spouse, and a member of the clergy. Suppose that the defendant, threatened with conviction for a serious crime and a lengthy term of imprisonment, seeks to compel the attorney, the spouse, or the member of the clergy to testify about the witness's admissions. Even though the constitutional rights of the defendant hang in the balance, the defendant's efforts to obtain the testimony would fail. The Court provides no good reason why the result in this case should not be the same.

## 5.   Racial Classification Benefiting Minorities

*Drawing Election Districts to Increase Minority Representation* (casebook p. 878)

In two cases—*Bethune Hill v. Virginia State of Elections* and *Cooper v. Harris*—the Supreme Court confronted whether and when the government can use race in drawing election districts. *Cooper v. Harris* seems particularly important because of the footnote in Justice Kagan's opinion that the use of race must meet strict scrutiny even if it is being considered as a proxy for political party affiliation. In light of this, *it* is unclear whether and to what extent *Easley v. Cromartie* (casebook p. 880) remains good law.

### BETHUNE-HILL v. VIRGINIA STATE BOARD OF ELECTIONS
137 S. Ct. 788 (2017)

Justice KENNEDY delivered the opinion of the Court.

This case addresses whether the Virginia state legislature's consideration of race in drawing new lines for 12 state legislative districts violated the Equal Protection Clause of the Fourteenth Amendment. After the 2010 census, some redistricting was required to ensure proper numerical apportionment for the Virginia House of Delegates. It is undisputed that the boundary lines for the 12 districts at issue were drawn with a goal of ensuring that each district would have a black voting-age population (BVAP) of at least 55%.

Certain voters challenged the new districts as unconstitutional racial gerrymanders. The United States District Court for the Eastern District of Virginia, constituted as a three-judge district court, rejected the challenges as to each of the 12 districts. As to 11 of the districts, the District Court concluded that the voters had not shown, as this Court's precedent requires, "that race was the predominant factor motivating the legislature's decision to place a significant number of voters within or without a particular district." *Miller v. Johnson* (1995). The District Court held that race predominates only where there is an " '*actual* conflict between traditional redistricting criteria and race,' " so it confined the predominance analysis to the portions of the new lines that appeared to deviate from traditional criteria, and found no violation. As to the remaining district, District 75, the District Court found that race did predominate. It concluded, however, that the lines were constitutional because the legislature's use of race was narrowly tailored to a compelling state interest. In particular, the District Court determined that the legislature had "good reasons to believe" that a 55% racial target was necessary in District 75 to avoid diminishing the ability of black voters to elect their preferred candidates, which at the time would have violated § 5 of the Voting Rights Act of 1965.

This Court now affirms as to District 75 and vacates and remands as to the remaining 11 districts.

# I

After the 2010 census, the Virginia General Assembly set out to redraw the legislative districts for the State Senate and House of Delegates in time for the 2011 elections. In February 2011, the House Committee on Privileges and Elections adopted a resolution establishing criteria to guide the redistricting process. Among those criteria were traditional redistricting factors such as compactness, contiguity of territory, and respect for communities of interest. But above those traditional objectives, the committee gave priority to two other goals. First, in accordance with the principle of one person, one vote, the committee resolved that "[t]he population of each district shall be as nearly equal to the population of every other district as practicable," with any deviations falling "within plus-or-minus one percent." Second, the committee resolved that the new map must comply with the "protections against . . . unwarranted retrogression" contained in § 5 of the Voting Rights Act. At the time, § 5 required covered jurisdictions, including Virginia, to preclear any change to a voting standard, practice, or procedure by showing federal authorities that the change would not have the purpose or effect of "diminishing the ability of [members of a minority group] to elect their preferred candidates of choice." After the redistricting process here was completed, this Court held that the coverage formula in § 4(b) of the Voting Rights Act no longer may be used to require preclearance under § 5.

The committee's criteria presented potential problems for 12 House districts. Under § 5 as Congress amended it in 2005, "[a] plan leads to impermissible retrogression when, compared to the plan currently in effect (typically called a 'benchmark plan'), the new plan diminishes the number of districts in which minority groups can 'elect their preferred candidates of choice' (often called 'ability-to-elect' districts)." The parties agree that the 12 districts at issue here, where minorities had constituted a majority of the voting-age population for many past elections, qualified as "ability-to-elect" districts. Most of the districts were underpopulated, however, so any new plan required moving significant numbers of new voters into these districts in order to comply with the principle of one person, one vote. Under the benchmark plan, the districts had BVAPs [Black Voting Age Populations] ranging from 62.7% down to 46.3%. Three districts had BVAPs below 55%.

Seeking to maintain minority voters' ability to elect their preferred candidates in these districts while complying with the one-person, one-vote criterion, legislators concluded that each of the 12 districts "needed to contain a BVAP of at least 55%." At trial, the parties disputed whether the 55% figure "was an aspiration or a target or a rule." But they did not dispute "the most important question—whether [the 55%] figure was used in drawing the Challenged Districts." The parties agreed, and the District Court found, "that the 55% BVAP figure was used in structuring the districts." In the enacted plan all 12 districts contained a BVAP greater than 55%.

II

Against the factual and procedural background set out above, it is now appropriate to consider the controlling legal principles in this case. The Equal Protection Clause prohibits a State, without sufficient justification, from "separat[ing] its citizens into different voting districts on the basis of race." The harms that flow from racial sorting "include being personally subjected to a racial classification as well as being represented by a legislator who believes his primary obligation is to represent only the members of a particular racial group." At the same time, courts must "exercise extraordinary caution in adjudicating claims that a State has drawn district lines on the basis of race." "Electoral districting is a most difficult subject for legislatures," requiring a delicate balancing of competing considerations. And "redistricting differs from other kinds of state decisionmaking in that the legislature always is *aware* of race when it draws district lines, just as it is aware of . . . a variety of other demographic factors."

In light of these considerations, this Court has held that a plaintiff alleging racial gerrymandering bears the burden "to show, either through circumstantial evidence of a district's shape and demographics or more direct evidence going to legislative purpose, that race was the predominant factor motivating the legislature's decision to place a significant number of voters within or without a particular district." To satisfy this burden, the plaintiff "must prove that the legislature subordinated traditional race-neutral districting principles . . . to racial considerations." The challengers contend that, in finding that race did not predominate in 11 of the 12 districts, the District Court misapplied controlling law in two principal ways. This Court considers them in turn.

A

The challengers first argue that the District Court misunderstood the relevant precedents when it required the challengers to establish, as a prerequisite to showing racial predominance, an actual conflict between the enacted plan and traditional redistricting principles. The Court agrees with the challengers on this point.

A threshold requirement that the enacted plan must conflict with traditional principles might have been reconcilable with this Court's case law at an earlier time. In *Shaw I,* the Court recognized a claim of racial gerrymandering for the first time. Certain language in *Shaw I* can be read to support requiring a challenger who alleges racial gerrymandering to show an actual conflict with traditional principles. The opinion stated, for example, that strict scrutiny applies to "redistricting legislation that is so bizarre on its face that it is unexplainable on grounds other than race." The opinion also stated that "reapportionment is one area in which appearances do matter."

The Court's opinion in *Miller,* however, clarified the racial predominance inquiry. In particular, it rejected the argument that, "regardless of the legislature's purposes, a plaintiff must demonstrate that a district's shape is so bizarre that it is unexplainable other than on the basis of race." The Court held to the contrary in language central to the instant case: "Shape is relevant not because bizarreness is a necessary element of the constitutional wrong or a threshold requirement of proof, but because it may be persuasive circumstantial evidence that race for its own sake, and not other districting principles, was the legislature's dominant and controlling rationale." Parties therefore "may rely on evidence other than bizarreness to establish race-based districting," and may show predominance "either through circumstantial evidence of a district's shape and demographics or more direct evidence going to legislative purpose."

The Court addressed racial gerrymandering and traditional redistricting factors again in *Shaw v. Hunt* (1996) (*Shaw II*). The Court there rejected the view of one of the dissents that "strict scrutiny does not apply where a State 'respects' or 'complies with traditional districting principles.'" Race may predominate even when a reapportionment plan respects traditional principles, the Court explained, if "[r]ace was the criterion that, in the State's view, could not be compromised," and race-neutral considerations "came into play only after the race-based decision had been made."

The State's theory in this case is irreconcilable with *Miller* and *Shaw II*. The State insists, for example, that the harm from racial gerrymandering lies not in racial line-drawing *per se* but in grouping voters of the same race together when they otherwise lack shared interests. But "the constitutional violation" in racial gerrymandering cases stems from the "racial purpose of state action, not its stark manifestation." The Equal Protection Clause does not prohibit misshapen districts. It prohibits unjustified racial classifications.

The State contends further that race does not have a prohibited effect on a district's lines if the legislature could have drawn the same lines in accordance with traditional criteria. That argument parallels the District Court's reasoning that a reapportionment plan is not an express racial classification unless a racial purpose is apparent from the face of the plan based on the irregular nature of the lines themselves. This is incorrect. The racial predominance inquiry concerns the actual considerations that provided the essential basis for the lines drawn, not *post hoc* justifications the legislature in theory could have used but in reality did not.

Traditional redistricting principles, moreover, are numerous and malleable. The District Court here identified no fewer than 11 race-neutral redistricting factors a legislature could consider, some of which are "surprisingly ethereal" and "admi[t] of degrees." By deploying those factors in various combinations and permutations, a State could construct a plethora of potential maps that look consistent with traditional, race-neutral principles. But if race for its own sake is the overriding reason for choosing one map over others, race still may predominate.

10For these reasons, a conflict or inconsistency between the enacted plan and traditional redistricting criteria is not a threshold requirement or a mandatory precondition in order for a challenger to establish a claim of racial gerrymandering. Of course, a conflict or inconsistency may be persuasive circumstantial evidence tending to show racial predomination, but there is no rule requiring challengers to present this kind of evidence in every case.

As a practical matter, in many cases, perhaps most cases, challengers will be unable to prove an unconstitutional racial gerrymander without evidence that the enacted plan conflicts with traditional redistricting criteria. In general, legislatures that engage in impermissible race-based redistricting will find it necessary to depart from traditional principles in order to do so. And, in the absence of a conflict with traditional principles, it may be difficult for challengers to find other evidence sufficient to show that race was the overriding factor causing neutral considerations to be cast aside. In fact, this Court to date has not affirmed a predominance finding, or remanded a case for a determination of predominance, without evidence that some district lines deviated from traditional principles. Yet the law responds to proper evidence and valid inferences in ever-changing circumstances, as it learns more about ways in which its commands are circumvented. So there may be cases where challengers will be able to establish racial predominance in the absence of an actual conflict by presenting direct evidence of the legislative purpose and intent or other compelling circumstantial evidence.

B

The challengers submit that the District Court erred further when it considered the legislature's racial motive only to the extent that the challengers identified deviations from traditional redistricting criteria that were attributable to race and not to some other factor. In the challengers' view, this approach foreclosed a holistic analysis of each district and led the District Court to give insufficient weight to the 55% BVAP target and other relevant evidence that race predominated. Again, this Court agrees.

As explained, showing a deviation from, or conflict with, traditional redistricting principles is not a necessary prerequisite to establishing racial predominance. But even where a challenger alleges a conflict, or succeeds in showing one, the court should not confine its analysis to the conflicting portions of the lines. That is because the basic unit of analysis for racial gerrymandering claims in general, and for the racial predominance inquiry in particular, is the district. Racial gerrymandering claims proceed "district-by-district." "We have consistently described a claim of racial gerrymandering as a claim that race was improperly used in the drawing of the boundaries of one or more *specific electoral districts.*" And *Miller*'s basic predominance test scrutinizes the legislature's motivation for placing "a significant number of voters within or without a particular district." Courts evaluating racial predominance therefore should not divorce any portion of the lines—whatever their relationship to traditional principles—from the rest of the district.

This is not to suggest that courts evaluating racial gerrymandering claims may not consider evidence pertaining to an area that is larger or smaller than the district at issue. The Court has recognized that "[v]oters, of course, can present statewide evidence in order to prove racial gerrymandering in a particular district." Districts share borders, after all, and a legislature may pursue a common redistricting policy toward multiple districts. Likewise, a legislature's race-based decisionmaking may be evident in a notable way in a particular part of a district. It follows that a court may consider evidence regarding certain portions of a district's lines, including portions that conflict with traditional redistricting principles.

The ultimate object of the inquiry, however, is the legislature's predominant motive for the design of the district as a whole. A court faced with a racial gerrymandering claim therefore must consider all of the lines of the district at issue; any explanation for a particular portion of the lines, moreover, must take account of the districtwide context. Concentrating on particular portions in isolation may obscure the significance of relevant districtwide evidence, such as stark splits in the racial composition of populations moved into and out of disparate parts of the district, or the use of an express racial target. A holistic analysis is necessary to give that kind of evidence its proper weight.

C

The challengers ask this Court not only to correct the District Court's racial predominance standard but also to apply that standard and conclude that race in fact did predominate in the 11 districts where the District Court held that it did not. For its part, the State asks the Court to hold that, even if race did predominate in these districts, the State's predominant use of race was narrowly tailored to the compelling interest in complying with § 5.

The Court declines these requests. "[O]urs is a court of final review and not first view." The District Court is best positioned to determine in the first instance the extent to which, under the proper standard, race directed the shape of these 11 districts. And if race did predominate, it is proper for the District Court to determine in the first instance whether strict scrutiny is satisfied. These matters are left for the District Court on remand.

## III

The Court now turns to the arguments regarding District 75. Where a challenger succeeds in establishing racial predominance, the burden shifts to the State to "demonstrate that its districting legislation is narrowly tailored to achieve a compelling interest." The District Court here determined that the State's predominant use of race in District 75 was narrowly tailored to achieve compliance with § 5. The challengers contest the finding of narrow tailoring, but they do not dispute that compliance with § 5 was a compelling interest at the relevant time. As in previous cases, therefore, the Court assumes, without deciding, that the State's interest in complying with the Voting Rights Act was compelling.

Turning to narrow tailoring, the Court explained the contours of that requirement in *Alabama*. When a State justifies the predominant use of race in redistricting on the basis of the need to comply with the Voting Rights Act, "the narrow tailoring requirement insists only that the legislature have a strong basis in evidence in support of the (race-based) choice that it has made." That standard does not require the State to show that its action was "actually . . . necessary" to avoid a statutory violation, so that, but for its use of race, the State would have lost in court. Rather, the requisite strong basis in evidence exists when the legislature has "*good reasons* to believe" it must use race in order to satisfy the Voting Rights Act, "even if a court does not find that the actions were necessary for statutory compliance."

The Court now finds no error in the District Court's conclusion that the State had sufficient grounds to determine that the race-based calculus it employed in District 75 was necessary to avoid violating § 5. As explained, § 5 at the time barred Virginia from adopting any districting change that would "have the effect of diminishing the ability of [members of a minority group] to elect their preferred candidates of choice." Determining what minority population percentage will satisfy that standard is a difficult task requiring, in the view of the Department of Justice, a "functional analysis of the electoral behavior within the particular . . . election district."

Under the facts found by the District Court, the legislature performed that kind of functional analysis of District 75 when deciding upon the

55% BVAP target. Redrawing this district presented a difficult task, and the result reflected the good-faith efforts of Delegate Jones and his colleagues to achieve an informed bipartisan consensus. In light of Delegate Jones' careful assessment of local conditions and structures, the State had a strong basis in evidence to believe a 55% BVAP floor was required to avoid retrogression.

## IV

The Court's holding in this case is controlled by precedent. The Court reaffirms the basic racial predominance analysis explained in *Miller* and *Shaw II,* and the basic narrow tailoring analysis explained in *Alabama*. The District Court's judgment as to District 75 is consistent with these principles. Applying these principles to the remaining 11 districts is entrusted to the District Court in the first instance.

Justice ALITO, concurring in part and concurring in the judgment.

I join the opinion of the Court insofar as it upholds the constitutionality of District 75. The districting plan at issue here was adopted prior to our decision in *Shelby County v. Holder* (2013), and therefore it is appropriate to apply the body of law in effect at that time. What is more, appellants have never contested the District Court's holding that compliance with § 5 of the Voting Rights Act was a compelling government interest for covered jurisdictions before our decision in *Shelby County*.

I concur in the judgment of the Court insofar as it vacates and remands the judgment below with respect to all the remaining districts. Unlike the Court, however, I would hold that all these districts must satisfy strict scrutiny. See *League of United Latin American Citizens v. Perry* (2006) (Scalia, J., concurring in judgment in part and dissenting in part) ("[W] hen a legislature intentionally creates a majority-minority district, race is necessarily its predominant motivation and strict scrutiny is therefore triggered").

Justice THOMAS, concurring in the judgment in part and dissenting in part.

Appellants contend that 12 of Virginia's state legislative districts are unconstitutional racial gerrymanders. The three-judge District Court rejected their challenge, holding that race was not the legislature's predominant motive in drawing 11 of the districts and that the remaining district survives strict scrutiny. I would reverse the District Court as to all 12 districts. I therefore concur in the judgment in part and dissent in part.

# I

I concur in the Court's judgment reversing the District Court's decision to uphold 11 of the 12 districts at issue in this case — House Districts 63, 69, 70, 71, 74, 77, 80, 89, 90, 92, and 95. I do not agree, however, with the Court's decision to leave open the question whether race predominated in those districts and, thus, whether they are subject to strict scrutiny. Appellees (hereinafter State) concede that the legislature intentionally drew all 12 districts as majority-black districts. That concession, in my view, mandates strict scrutiny as to each district.

# II

I disagree with the Court's judgment with respect to the remaining district, District 75. The majority affirms the District Court's holding that District 75 is subject to strict scrutiny. With this I agree, because, as with the other 11 districts, the State conceded that it intentionally drew District 75 as a majority-black district.

I disagree, however, with the majority's determination that District 75 satisfies strict scrutiny. This Court has held that a State may draw distinctions among its citizens based on race only when it "is pursuing a compelling state interest" and has chosen "narrowly tailored" means to accomplish that interest. The State asserts that it used race in drawing District 75 to further a "compelling interest in complying with Section 5 of the [Voting Rights Act of 1965]." And it argues that, based on its "good-faith functional analysis" of the district, it narrowly tailored its use of race to achieve that interest. In my view, the State has neither asserted a compelling state interest nor narrowly tailored its use of race.

## A

As an initial matter, the majority errs by "assum[ing], without deciding, that the State's interest in complying with the Voting Rights Act was compelling." To be sure, this Court has previously assumed that a State has a compelling interest in complying with the Voting Rights Act. But it has done so only in cases in which it has not upheld the redistricting plan at issue. This Court has never, before today, assumed a compelling state interest while upholding a state redistricting plan. Indeed, I know of no other case, in any context, in which the Court has assumed away part of the State's burden to justify its intentional use of race. This should not be the first. I would hold that complying with § 5 of the Voting Rights Act is not a compelling interest.

"[C]ompliance with federal antidiscrimination laws cannot justify race-based districting where the challenged district was not reasonably necessary under a *constitutional* reading and application of those laws." Because, in my view, § 5 is unconstitutional, I would hold that a State does not have a compelling interest in complying with it.

B

Even if compliance with § 5 were a compelling interest, the State failed to narrowly tailor its use of race to further that interest. This Court has explained that "[a]ny preference based on racial or ethnic criteria must necessarily receive a most searching examination." This exacting scrutiny makes sense because "[d]iscrimination on the basis of race" is "odious in all aspects." Accordingly, a State's use of race must bear " 'the most exact connection' " to the compelling state interest. In the context of redistricting, the redistricting map must, "at a minimum," actually "remedy the anticipated violation" or "achieve compliance" with the Voting Rights Act.

I have serious doubts about the Court's standard for narrow tailoring. [This] approach to narrow tailoring — deferring to a State's belief that it has good reasons to use race — is "strict" in name only. Applying the proper narrow-tailoring standard for state classifications based on race, I conclude that the State did not narrowly tailor its use of race to comply with § 5. As the majority recognizes, § 5 requires a state redistricting plan to maintain the black population's ability to elect the candidate of its choice in the district at issue — in other words, the State must "avoid retrogression" in the new district.

In reaching these conclusions, I recognize that this Court is at least as responsible as the state legislature for these racially gerrymandered districts. As explained above, this Court has repeatedly failed to decide whether compliance with the Voting Rights Act is a compelling governmental interest. Indeed, this Court has refused even to decide whether § 5 is constitutional, despite having twice taken cases to decide that question. As a result, the Court has left the State without clear guidance about its redistricting obligations under § 5.

This Court has put the State in a similar bind with respect to narrow tailoring. To comply with § 5, a State necessarily must make a deliberate and precise effort to sort its citizens on the basis of their race. But that result is fundamentally at odds with our "color-blind" Constitution, which "neither knows nor tolerates classes among citizens." That contradiction illustrates the perversity of the Court's jurisprudence in this area as well as the uncomfortable position in which the State might find itself.

Despite my sympathy for the State, I cannot ignore the Constitution's clear prohibition on state-sponsored race discrimination. "The Constitution abhors classifications based on race, not only because those classifications can harm favored races or are based on illegitimate motives, but also because every time the government places citizens on racial registers . . . , it demeans us all." This prohibition was "[p]urchased at the price of immeasurable human suffering," and it "reflects our Nation's understanding that such classifications ultimately have a destructive impact on the individual and our society." I respectfully dissent from the Court's judgment as to District 75.

***

COOPER v. HARRIS
137 S. Ct. 1455 (2017)

Justice KAGAN delivered the opinion of the Court.

The Constitution entrusts States with the job of designing congressional districts. But it also imposes an important constraint: A State may not use race as the predominant factor in drawing district lines unless it has a compelling reason. In this case, a three-judge District Court ruled that North Carolina officials violated that bar when they created two districts whose voting-age populations were majority black. Applying a deferential standard of review to the factual findings underlying that decision, we affirm.

I

A

The Equal Protection Clause of the Fourteenth Amendment limits racial gerrymanders in legislative districting plans. It prevents a State, in the absence of "sufficient justification," from "separating its citizens into different voting districts on the basis of race." When a voter sues state officials for drawing such race-based lines, our decisions call for a two-step analysis.

First, the plaintiff must prove that "race was the predominant factor motivating the legislature's decision to place a significant number of voters within or without a particular district." That entails demonstrating that the legislature "subordinated" other factors—compactness, respect for political subdivisions, partisan advantage, what have you—to "racial considerations." The plaintiff may make the required showing through "direct evidence" of legislative intent, "circumstantial evidence of a district's shape and demographics," or a mix of both.

Second, if racial considerations predominated over others, the design of the district must withstand strict scrutiny. The burden thus shifts to the State to prove that its race-based sorting of voters serves a "compelling interest" and is "narrowly tailored" to that end. This Court has long assumed that one compelling interest is complying with operative provisions of the Voting Rights Act of 1965 (VRA or Act). When a State invokes the VRA to justify race-based districting, it must show (to meet the "narrow tailoring" requirement) that it had "a strong basis in evidence" for concluding that the statute required its action. Or said otherwise, the State must establish that it had "good reasons" to think that it would transgress the Act if it did *not* draw race-based district lines. That "strong basis" (or "good reasons") standard gives States "breathing room" to adopt reasonable compliance measures that may prove, in perfect hindsight, not to have been needed.

A district court's assessment of a districting plan, in accordance with the two-step inquiry just described, warrants significant deference on appeal to this Court. We of course retain full power to correct a court's errors of law, at either stage of the analysis. But the court's findings of fact—most notably, as to whether racial considerations predominated in drawing district lines—are subject to review only for clear error. Under that standard, we may not reverse just because we "would have decided the [matter] differently." A finding that is "plausible" in light of the full record—even if another is equally or more so—must govern.

B

This case concerns North Carolina's most recent redrawing of two congressional districts, both of which have long included substantial populations of black voters. In its current incarnation, District 1 is anchored in the northeastern part of the State, with appendages stretching both south and west (the latter into Durham). District 12 begins in the south-central part of the State (where it takes in a large part of Charlotte) and then travels northeast, zig-zagging much of the way to the State's northern border. Both have quite the history before this Court.

Registered voters in the two districts (David Harris and Christine Bowser, here called "the plaintiffs") brought this suit against North Carolina officials (collectively, "the State" or "North Carolina"), complaining of impermissible racial gerrymanders. After a bench trial, a three-judge District Court held both districts unconstitutional. All the judges agreed that racial considerations predominated in the design of District 1. And in then applying strict scrutiny, all rejected the State's argument that it had a "strong basis" for thinking that the VRA compelled such a race-based drawing of District 1's lines. As for District 12, a majority of the panel held that "race predominated" over all other factors, including partisanship.

[II]

[W]e turn to the merits of this case, beginning (appropriately enough) with District 1. As noted above, the court below found that race furnished the predominant rationale for that district's redesign. And it held that the State's interest in complying with the VRA could not justify that consideration of race. We uphold both conclusions.

Uncontested evidence in the record shows that the State's mapmakers, in considering District 1, purposefully established a racial target: African–Americans should make up no less than a majority of the voting-age population. The result is a district with stark racial borders: Within the same counties, the portions that fall inside District 1 have black populations two to three times larger than the portions placed in neighboring districts. Faced with this body of evidence — showing an announced racial target that subordinated other districting criteria and produced boundaries amplifying divisions between blacks and whites — the District Court did not clearly err in finding that race predominated in drawing District 1. Indeed, as all three judges recognized, the court could hardly have concluded anything but.

The more substantial question is whether District 1 can survive the strict scrutiny applied to racial gerrymanders. As noted earlier, we have long assumed that complying with the VRA is a compelling interest. And we have held that race-based districting is narrowly tailored to that objective if a State had "good reasons" for thinking that the Act demanded such steps.

This Court identified, in *Thornburg v. Gingles,* three threshold conditions for proving vote dilution under § 2 of the VRA. First, a "minority group" must be "sufficiently large and geographically compact to constitute a majority" in some reasonably configured legislative district. Second, the minority group must be "politically cohesive." And third, a district's white majority must "vote [ ] sufficiently as a bloc" to usually "defeat the minority's preferred candidate." *Ibid.* Those three showings, we have explained, are needed to establish that "the minority [group] has the potential to elect a representative of its own choice" in a possible district, but that racially polarized voting prevents it from doing so in the district as actually drawn because it is "submerg[ed] in a larger white voting population." If a State has good reason to think that all the *"Gingles* preconditions" are met, then so too it has good reason to believe that § 2 requires drawing a majority-minority district. But if not, then not.

Here, electoral history provided no evidence that a § 2 plaintiff could demonstrate the third *Gingles* prerequisite — effective white bloc-voting. For most of the twenty years prior to the new plan's adoption, African-Americans had made up less than a majority of District 1's voters, but their preferred candidates scored consistent victories. District 1 thus functioned as a "crossover" district, in which members of the majority help a "large enough" minority to elect its candidate of choice. *Bartlett* v. *Strickland*, 556 U.S. 1 (plurality opinion). So experience gave the State no reason to think that the VRA required it to ramp up District 1's BVAP.

Thus, North Carolina's belief that it was compelled to redraw District 1 (a successful crossover district) as a majority-minority district rested not on a "strong basis in evidence," but instead on a pure error of law. In sum: Although States enjoy leeway to take race-based actions reasonably judged necessary under a proper interpretation of the VRA, that latitude cannot rescue District 1. We by no means "insist that a state legislature, when redistricting, determine *precisely* what percent minority population [§ 2 of the VRA] demands." But neither will we approve a racial gerrymander whose necessity is supported by no evidence and whose *raison d'être* is a legal mistake. Accordingly, we uphold the District Court's conclusion that North Carolina's use of race as the predominant factor in designing District 1 does not withstand strict scrutiny.

[III]

We now look west to District 12, making its fifth(!) appearance before this Court. [T]he State altogether denied that racial considerations accounted for (or, indeed, played the slightest role in) District 12's redesign. According to the State's version of events, Senator Rucho, Representative Lewis, and Dr. Hofeller moved voters in and out of the district as part of a "strictly" political gerrymander, without regard to race. The mapmakers drew their lines, in other words, to "pack" District 12 with Democrats, not African-Americans. After hearing evidence supporting both parties' accounts, the District Court accepted the plaintiffs'.

Getting to the bottom of a dispute like this one poses special challenges for a trial court. In the more usual case alleging a racial gerrymander — where no one has raised a partisanship defense — the court can make real headway by exploring the challenged district's conformity to traditional districting principles, such as compactness and respect for county lines. But such evidence loses much of its value when the State asserts partisanship as a defense, because a bizarre shape — as of the new District 12 — can arise from a "political motivation" as well as a racial one. And crucially, political and racial reasons are capable of yielding similar oddities in a district's boundaries. That is because, of course, "racial identification is highly correlated with political affiliation." As a result of those redistricting realities, a trial court has a formidable task: It must make "a sensitive inquiry" into all "circumstantial and direct evidence of intent" to assess whether the plaintiffs have managed to disentangle race from politics and prove that the former drove a district's lines.[1]

Our job is different — and generally easier. As described earlier, we review a district court's finding as to racial predominance only for clear error, except when the court made a legal mistake. Under that standard of review, we affirm the court's finding so long as it is "plausible"; we reverse only when "left with the definite and firm conviction that a mistake has been committed." And in deciding which side of that line to come down on, we give singular deference to a trial court's judgments about the credibility of witnesses. That is proper, we have explained, because the various cues that "bear so heavily on the listener's understanding of and belief in what is said" are lost on an appellate court later sifting through a paper record.

In light of those principles, we uphold the District Court's finding of racial predominance respecting District 12. The evidence offered at trial, including live witness testimony subject to credibility determinations, adequately supports the conclusion that race, not politics, accounted for the district's reconfiguration. And no error of law infected that judgment: Contrary to North Carolina's view, the District Court had no call to dismiss this challenge just because the plaintiffs did not proffer an alternative design for District 12 as circumstantial evidence of the legislature's intent.

---

1. As earlier noted, that inquiry is satisfied when legislators have "place[d] a significant number of voters within or without" a district predominantly because of their race, regardless of their ultimate objective in taking that step. So, for example, if legislators use race as their predominant districting criterion with the end goal of advancing their partisan interests — perhaps thinking that a proposed district is more "sellable" as a race-based VRA compliance measure than as a political gerrymander and will accomplish much the same thing — their action still triggers strict scrutiny. In other words, the sorting of voters on the grounds of their race remains suspect even if race is meant to function as a proxy for other (including political) characteristics. [Footnote by Justice KAGAN]

The State mounts a final, legal rather than factual, attack on the District Court's finding of racial predominance. When race and politics are competing explanations of a district's lines, argues North Carolina, the party challenging the district must introduce a particular kind of circumstantial evidence: "an alternative [map] that achieves the legislature's political objectives while improving racial balance." That is true, the State says, irrespective of what other evidence is in the case — so even if the plaintiff offers powerful direct proof that the legislature adopted the map it did for racial reasons. Because the plaintiffs here (as all agree) did not present such a counter-map, North Carolina concludes that they cannot prevail. The dissent echoes that argument.

We have no doubt that an alternative districting plan, of the kind North Carolina describes, can serve as key evidence in a race-versus-politics dispute. One, often highly persuasive way to disprove a State's contention that politics drove a district's lines is to show that the legislature had the capacity to accomplish all its partisan goals without moving so many members of a minority group into the district. If you were *really* sorting by political behavior instead of skin color (so the argument goes) you would have done — or, at least, could just as well have done — *this*. Such would-have, could-have, and (to round out the set) should-have arguments are a familiar means of undermining a claim that an action was based on a permissible, rather than a prohibited, ground.

But they are hardly the *only* means. Suppose that the plaintiff in a dispute like this one introduced scores of leaked emails from state officials instructing their mapmaker to pack as many black voters as possible into a district, or telling him to make sure its BVAP hit 75%. Based on such evidence, a court could find that racial rather than political factors predominated in a district's design, with or without an alternative map. And so too in cases lacking that kind of smoking gun, as long as the evidence offered satisfies the plaintiff's burden of proof. Similarly, it does not matter in this case, where the plaintiffs' introduction of mostly direct and some circumstantial evidence — documents issued in the redistricting process, testimony of government officials, expert analysis of demographic patterns — gave the District Court a sufficient basis, sans any map, to resolve the race-or-politics question.

plaintiff's task, in other words, is simply to persuade the trial court — without any special evidentiary prerequisite — that race (not politics) was the "predominant consideration in deciding to place a significant number of voters within or without a particular district." That burden of proof, we have often held, is "demanding." And because that is so, a plaintiff will sometimes need an alternative map, as a practical matter, to make his case. But in no area of our equal protection law have we forced plaintiffs to submit one particular form of proof to prevail. Nor would it make sense to do so here. The Equal Protection Clause prohibits the unjustified drawing of district lines based on race. An alternative map is merely an evidentiary tool to show that such a substantive violation has occurred; neither its presence nor its absence can itself resolve a racial gerrymandering claim.

## V

Applying a clear error standard, we uphold the District Court's conclusions that racial considerations predominated in designing both District 1 and District 12. For District 12, that is all we must do, because North Carolina has made no attempt to justify race-based districting there. For District 1, we further uphold the District Court's decision that § 2 of the VRA gave North Carolina no good reason to reshuffle voters because of their race.

Justice THOMAS, concurring.

I join the opinion of the Court because it correctly applies our precedents under the Constitution and the Voting Rights Act of 1965 (VRA). I write briefly to explain the additional grounds on which I would affirm the three-judge District Court and to note my agreement, in particular, with the Court's clear-error analysis.

As to District 1, I think North Carolina's concession that it created the district as a majority-black district is by itself sufficient to trigger strict scrutiny. I also think that North Carolina cannot satisfy strict scrutiny based on its efforts to comply with § 2 of the VRA. In my view, § 2 does not apply to redistricting and therefore cannot justify a racial gerrymander.

As to District 12, I agree with the Court that the District Court did not clearly err when it determined that race was North Carolina's predominant motive in drawing the district. This is the same conclusion I reached when we last reviewed District 12. *Easley v. Cromartie* (2001) (*Cromartie II*) (dissenting opinion).

Justice ALITO, with whom THE CHIEF JUSTICE and Justice KENNEDY join, concurring in the judgment in part and dissenting in part.

A precedent of this Court should not be treated like a disposable household item—say, a paper plate or napkin—to be used once and then tossed in the trash. But that is what the Court does today in its decision regarding North Carolina's 12th Congressional District: The Court junks a rule adopted in a prior, remarkably similar challenge to this very same congressional district.

In *Easley v. Cromartie* (2001) (*Cromartie II* ), the Court considered the constitutionality of the version of District 12 that was adopted in 1997. That district had the same basic shape as the district now before us, and the challengers argued that the legislature's predominant reason for adopting this configuration was race. The State responded that its motive was not race but politics. Its objective, the State insisted, was to create a district in which the Democratic candidate would win. Rejecting that explanation, a three-judge court found that the legislature's predominant motive was racial, specifically to pack African–Americans into District 12. But this Court held that this finding of fact was clearly erroneous.

A critical factor in our analysis was the failure of those challenging the district to come forward with an alternative redistricting map that served the legislature's political objective as well as the challenged version without producing the same racial effects. Noting that race and party affiliation in North Carolina were "highly correlated," we laid down this rule:

"In a case such as this one . . . , the party attacking the legislatively drawn boundaries must show at the least that the legislature could have achieved its legitimate political objectives in alternative ways that are comparably consistent with traditional districting principles. That party must also show that those districting alternatives would have brought about significantly greater racial balance. Appellees failed to make any such showing here."

Now, District 12 is back before us. After the 2010 census, the North Carolina Legislature, with the Republicans in the majority, drew the present version of District 12. The challengers contend that this version violates equal protection because the predominant motive of the legislature was racial: to pack the district with African–American voters. The legislature responds that its objective was political: to pack the district with Democrats and thus to increase the chances of Republican candidates in neighboring districts.

You might think that the *Cromartie II* rule would be equally applicable in this case, which does not differ in any relevant particular, but the majority executes a stunning about-face. Now, the challengers' failure to produce an alternative map that meets the *Cromartie II* test is inconsequential. It simply "does not matter."

This is not the treatment of precedent that state legislatures have the right to expect from this Court. The failure to produce an alternative map doomed the challengers in *Cromartie II,* and the same should be true now. Partisan gerrymandering is always unsavory, but that is not the issue here. The issue is whether District 12 was drawn predominantly because of race. The record shows that it was not.

The alternative-map requirement deserves better. It is a logical response to the difficult problem of distinguishing between racial and political motivations when race and political party preference closely correlate. This is a problem with serious institutional and federalism implications. When a federal court says that race was a legislature's predominant purpose in drawing a district, it accuses the legislature of "offensive and demeaning" conduct. Indeed, we have said that racial gerrymanders "bea[r] an uncomfortable resemblance to political apartheid." That is a grave accusation to level against a state legislature.

In addition, "[f]ederal-court review of districting legislation represents a serious intrusion on the most vital of local functions" because "[i]t is well settled that reapportionment is primarily the duty and responsibility of the State." When a federal court finds that race predominated in the redistricting process, it inserts itself into that process. That is appropriate — indeed, constitutionally required — if the legislature truly did draw district boundaries on the basis of race. But if a court mistakes a political gerrymander for a racial gerrymander, it illegitimately invades a traditional domain of state authority, usurping the role of a State's elected representatives. This does violence to both the proper role of the Judiciary and the powers reserved to the States under the Constitution.

There is a final, often-unstated danger where race and politics correlate: that the federal courts will be transformed into weapons of political warfare. Unless courts "exercise extraordinary caution" in distinguishing race-based redistricting from politics-based redistricting, they will invite the losers in the redistricting process to seek to obtain in court what they could not achieve in the political arena. If the majority party draws districts to favor itself, the minority party can deny the majority its political victory by prevailing on a racial gerrymandering claim. Even if the minority party loses in court, it can exact a heavy price by using the judicial process to engage in political trench warfare for years on end.

The majority nevertheless absolves the challengers of their failure to submit an alternative map. It argues that an alternative map cannot be "the *only* means" of proving racial predominance, and it concludes from this that an alternative map "does not matter in this case." But even if there are cases in which a plaintiff could prove a racial gerrymandering claim without an alternative map, they would be exceptional ones in which the evidence of racial predominance is overwhelming. This most definitely is not one of those cases, and the plaintiffs' failure to produce an alternative map mandates reversal. Moreover, even in an exceptional case, the absence of such a map would still be strong evidence that a district's boundaries were determined by politics rather than race.

Even if we set aside the challengers' failure to submit an alternative map, the District Court's finding that race predominated in the drawing of District 12 is clearly erroneous. The State offered strong and coherent evidence that politics, not race, was the legislature's predominant aim, and the evidence supporting the District Court's contrary finding is weak and manifestly inadequate in light of the high evidentiary standard that our cases require challengers to meet in order to prove racial predominance.

# Chapter 8

# Fundamental Rights Under Due Process and Equal Protection

## C. Constitutional Protection for Family Autonomy

### 1. The Right to Marry (casebook p. 955)

In *Obergefell v. Hodges* (casebook p. 967), the Court held that gay and lesbian

Couples have the same right to marry as opposite sex couples. In *Pavan v. Smith*, the Court reversed – without briefs or oral arguments – an Arkansas Supreme Court decision preventing lesbian couples from listing both parents on the birth certificate. But three justices dissented.

### PAVAN v. SMITH
137 S. Ct. ___ (2017)

PER CURIAM.

As this Court explained in *Obergefell v. Hodges* (2015), the Constitution entitles same-sex couples to civil marriage "on the same terms and conditions as opposite-sex couples." In the decision below, the Arkansas Supreme Court considered the effect of that holding on the State's rules governing the issuance of birth certificates. When a married woman gives birth in Arkansas, state law generally requires the name of the mother's male spouse to appear on the child's birth certificate—regardless of his biological relationship to the child. According to the court below, however, Arkansas need not extend that rule to similarly situated same-sex couples: The State need not, in other words, issue birth certificates including the female spouses of women who give birth in the State. Because that differential treatment infringes *Obergefell*'s commitment to provide same-sex couples "the constellation of benefits that the States have linked to marriage," we reverse the state court's judgment.

The petitioners here are two married same-sex couples who conceived children through anonymous sperm donation. Leigh and Jana Jacobs were married in Iowa in 2010, and Terrah and Marisa Pavan were married in New Hampshire in 2011. Leigh and Terrah each gave birth to a child in Arkansas in 2015. When it came time to secure birth certificates for the newborns, each couple filled out paperwork listing both spouses as parents—Leigh and Jana in one case, Terrah and Marisa in the other. Both times, however, the Arkansas Department of Health issued certificates bearing only the birth mother's name.

The department's decision rested on a provision of Arkansas law, Ark. Code § 20–18–401(2014), that specifies which individuals will appear as parents on a child's state-issued birth certificate. "For the purposes of birth registration," that statute says, "the mother is deemed to be the woman who gives birth to the child." And "[i]f the mother was married at the time of either conception or birth," the statute instructs that "the name of [her] husband shall be entered on the certificate as the father of the child." There are some limited exceptions to the latter rule—for example, another man may appear on the birth certificate if the "mother" and "husband" and "putative father" all file affidavits vouching for the putative father's paternity. But as all parties agree, the requirement that a married woman's husband appear on her child's birth certificate applies in cases where the couple conceived by means of artificial insemination with the help of an anonymous sperm donor.

The Jacobses and Pavans brought this suit in Arkansas state court against the director of the Arkansas Department of Health—seeking, among other things, a declaration that the State's birth-certificate law violates the Constitution. The trial court agreed, holding that the relevant portions of § 20–18–401 are inconsistent with *Obergefell* because they "categorically prohibi[t] every same-sex married couple . . . from enjoying the same spousal benefits which are available to every opposite-sex married couple." But a divided Arkansas Supreme Court reversed that judgment, concluding that the statute "pass[es] constitutional muster." In that court's view, "the statute centers on the relationship of the biological mother and the biological father to the child, not on the marital relationship of husband and wife," and so it "does not run afoul of *Obergefell*."

The Arkansas Supreme Court's decision, we conclude, denied married same-sex couples access to the "constellation of benefits that the Stat[e] ha[s] linked to marriage." As already explained, when a married woman in Arkansas conceives a child by means of artificial insemination, the State will—indeed, *must*—list the name of her male spouse on the child's birth certificate. And yet state law, as interpreted by the court below, allows Arkansas officials in those very same circumstances to omit a married woman's female spouse from her child's birth certificate. As a result, same-sex parents in Arkansas lack the same right as opposite-sex parents to be listed on a child's birth certificate, a document often used for important transactions like making medical decisions for a child or enrolling a child in school.

*Obergefell* proscribes such disparate treatment. As we explained there, a State may not "exclude same-sex couples from civil marriage on the same terms and conditions as opposite-sex couples." Indeed, in listing those terms and conditions — the "rights, benefits, and responsibilities" to which same-sex couples, no less than opposite-sex couples, must have access — we expressly identified "birth and death certificates." That was no accident: Several of the plaintiffs in *Obergefell* challenged a State's refusal to recognize their same-sex spouses on their children's birth certificates. In considering those challenges, we held the relevant state laws unconstitutional to the extent they treated same-sex couples differently from opposite-sex couples. That holding applies with equal force to § 20–18–401.

Arkansas has thus chosen to make its birth certificates more than a mere marker of biological relationships: The State uses those certificates to give married parents a form of legal recognition that is not available to unmarried parents. Having made that choice, Arkansas may not, consistent with *Obergefell*, deny married same-sex couples that recognition.

Justice GORSUCH, with whom Justice THOMAS and Justice ALITO join, dissenting.

Summary reversal is usually reserved for cases where "the law is settled and stable, the facts are not in dispute, and the decision below is clearly in error." Respectfully, I don't believe this case meets that standard.

To be sure, *Obergefell* addressed the question whether a State must recognize same-sex marriages. But nothing in *Obergefell* spoke (let alone clearly) to the question whether § 20–18–401 of the Arkansas Code, or a state supreme court decision upholding it, must go. The statute in question establishes a set of rules designed to ensure that the biological parents of a child are listed on the child's birth certificate. Before the state supreme court, the State argued that rational reasons exist for a biology based birth registration regime, reasons that in no way offend *Obergefell* — like ensuring government officials can identify public health trends and helping individuals determine their biological lineage, citizenship, or susceptibility to genetic disorders. In an opinion that did not in any way seek to defy but rather earnestly engage *Obergefell*, the state supreme court agreed. And it is very hard to see what is wrong with this conclusion for, just as the state court recognized, nothing in *Obergefell* indicates that a birth registration regime based on biology, one no doubt with many analogues across the country and throughout history, offends the Constitution. To the contrary, to the extent they speak to the question at all, this Court's precedents suggest just the opposite conclusion. Neither does anything in today's opinion purport to identify any constitutional problem with a biology based birth registration regime. So whatever else we might do with this case, summary reversal would not exactly seem the obvious course.

Given all this, it seems far from clear what here warrants the strong medicine of summary reversal. Indeed, it is not even clear what the Court expects to happen on remand that hasn't happened already. The Court does not offer any remedial suggestion, and none leaps to mind. Perhaps the state supreme court could memorialize the State's concession on § 9–10–201, even though that law wasn't fairly challenged and such a chore is hardly the usual reward for seeking faithfully to apply, not evade, this Court's mandates.

## D.   *Gender Classifications*

## 3.   **Gender Classifications Benefiting Women (casebook p. 914)**

In *Sessions v. Morales-Santana,* 137 S. Ct. 1678 (2017), the Court considered a federal immigration statute that treats mothers and fathers differently with regard to acquiring United States citizenship. For a child born abroad when one parent is a citizen and one not a citizen, the law required presence in the United States for 10 years before the child's birth in order for the child to be deemed a United States citizen. Congress waived this requirement for women, but not for men. The Supreme Court found this unconstitutional as a denial of equal protection. Interestingly, the Court said that the appropriate remedy for such an equal protection violation is to treat mothers and fathers the same, not necessarily to waive this for men.

# Chapter 9

# First Amendment: Freedom of Expression

## B. Free Speech Methodology

### 1. The Distinction Between Content-Based and Content-Neutral Laws (casebook p. 1244)

In *Matal v. Tam*, the Court considered whether it violated the First Amendment to deny a band the ability to register its name as a trademark because it was racially offensive. Notice all of the justices agree that this is unconstitutional because it is viewpoint discrimination.

### MATAL v. TAM
138 S. Ct. ___ (2017)

Justice ALITO announced the judgment of the Court and delivered the opinion of the Court with respect to Parts I, II, and III–A, and an opinion with respect to Parts III–B, III–C, and IV, in which THE CHIEF JUSTICE, Justice THOMAS, and Justice BREYER join.

This case concerns a dance-rock band's application for federal trademark registration of the band's name, "The Slants." "Slants" is a derogatory term for persons of Asian descent, and members of the band are Asian–Americans. But the band members believe that by taking that slur as the name of their group, they will help to "reclaim" the term and drain its denigrating force.

The Patent and Trademark Office (PTO) denied the application based on a provision of federal law prohibiting the registration of trademarks that may "disparage . . . or bring . . . into contemp[t] or disrepute" any "persons, living or dead." We now hold that this provision violates the Free Speech Clause of the First Amendment. It offends a bedrock First Amendment principle: Speech may not be banned on the ground that it expresses ideas that offend.

I

"The principle underlying trademark protection is that distinctive marks—words, names, symbols, and the like—can help distinguish a particular artisan's goods from those of others." A trademark "designate [s] the goods as the product of a particular trader" and "protect[s] his good will against the sale of another's product as his." It helps consumers identify goods and services that they wish to purchase, as well as those they want to avoid.

"[F]ederal law does not create trademarks." Trademarks and their precursors have ancient origins, and trademarks were protected at common law and in equity at the time of the founding of our country. The foundation of current federal trademark law is the Lanham Act, enacted in 1946. Under the Lanham Act, trademarks that are "used in commerce" may be placed on the "principal register," that is, they may be federally registered. There are now more than two million marks that have active federal certificates of registration. This system of federal registration helps to ensure that trademarks are fully protected and supports the free flow of commerce. "[N]ational protection of trademarks is desirable," we have explained, "because trademarks foster competition and the maintenance of quality by securing to the producer the benefits of good reputation."

Without federal registration, a valid trademark may still be used in commerce. And an unregistered trademark can be enforced against would-be infringers in several ways. Most important, even if a trademark is not federally registered, it may still be enforceable under § 43(a) of the Lanham Act, which creates a federal cause of action for trademark infringement. And an unregistered trademark can be enforced under state common law, or if it has been registered in a State, under that State's registration system.

Federal registration, however, "confers important legal rights and benefits on trademark owners who register their marks." Registration on the principal register (1) "serves as 'constructive notice of the registrant's claim of ownership' of the mark,"; (2) "is 'prima facie evidence of the validity of the registered mark and of the registration of the mark, of the owner's ownership of the mark, and of the owner's exclusive right to use the registered mark in commerce on or in connection with the goods or services specified in the certificate,'" and (3) can make a mark "'incontestable'" once a mark has been registered for five years. Registration also enables the trademark holder "to stop the importation into the United States of articles bearing an infringing mark."

The Lanham Act contains provisions that bar certain trademarks from the principal register. For example, a trademark cannot be registered if it is "merely descriptive or deceptively misdescriptive" of goods, or if it is so similar to an already registered trademark or trade name that it is "likely . . . to cause confusion, or to cause mistake, or to deceive." At issue in this case is one such provision, which we will call "the disparagement clause." This provision prohibits the registration of a trademark "which may disparage . . . persons, living or dead, institutions, beliefs, or national symbols, or bring them into contempt, or disrepute." § 1052(a). This clause appeared in the original Lanham Act and has remained the same to this day.

Simon Tam is the lead singer of "The Slants." He chose this moniker in order to "reclaim" and "take ownership" of stereotypes about people of Asian ethnicity. The group "draws inspiration for its lyrics from childhood slurs and mocking nursery rhymes" and has given its albums names such as "The Yellow Album" and "Slanted Eyes, Slanted Hearts."

Tam sought federal registration of "THE SLANTS," on the principal register, but an examining attorney at the PTO rejected the request, finding that "there is . . . a substantial composite of persons who find the term in the applied-for mark offensive." The examining attorney relied in part on the fact that "numerous dictionaries define 'slants' or 'slant-eyes' as a derogatory or offensive term." The examining attorney also relied on a finding that "the band's name has been found offensive numerous times"—citing a performance that was canceled because of the band's moniker and the fact that "several bloggers and commenters to articles on the band have indicated that they find the term and the applied-for mark offensive." *Id.*, at 29–30.

Tam contested the denial of registration before the examining attorney and before the PTO's Trademark Trial and Appeal Board (TTAB) but to no avail.

## II

[In Part II of the opinion the Court held that the statutory provision does prohibit trademarks that are disparaging to racial groups.]

## III

Because the disparagement clause applies to marks that disparage the members of a racial or ethnic group, we must decide whether the clause violates the Free Speech Clause of the First Amendment. And at the

outset, we must consider three arguments that would either eliminate any
First Amendment protection or result in highly permissive rational-basis
review. Specifically, the Government contends (1) that trademarks are
government speech, not private speech, (2) that trademarks are a form of
government subsidy, and (3) that the constitutionality of the disparagement clause should be tested under a new "government-program" doctrine. We address each of these arguments below.

A

The First Amendment prohibits Congress and other government entities
and actors from "abridging the freedom of speech"; the First Amendment
does not say that Congress and other government entities must abridge
their own ability to speak freely. And our cases recognize that "[t]he
Free Speech Clause . . . does not regulate government speech." When
a government entity embarks on a course of action, it necessarily takes
a particular viewpoint and rejects others. The Free Speech Clause does
not require government to maintain viewpoint neutrality when its officers
and employees speak about that venture.

But while the government-speech doctrine is important—indeed,
essential—it is a doctrine that is susceptible to dangerous misuse. If private speech could be passed off as government speech by simply affixing
a government seal of approval, government could silence or muffle the
expression of disfavored viewpoints. For this reason, we must exercise
great caution before extending our government-speech precedents.

At issue here is the content of trademarks that are registered by the
PTO, an arm of the Federal Government. The Federal Government does
not dream up these marks, and it does not edit marks submitted for registration. Except as required by the statute involved here, an examiner
may not reject a mark based on the viewpoint that it appears to express.
Thus, unless that section is thought to apply, an examiner does not inquire
whether any viewpoint conveyed by a mark is consistent with Government
policy or whether any such viewpoint is consistent with that expressed by
other marks already on the principal register. Instead, if the mark meets
the Lanham Act's viewpoint-neutral requirements, registration is mandatory. And if an examiner finds that a mark is eligible for placement on
the principal register, that decision is not reviewed by any higher official
unless the registration is challenged.

In light of all this, it is far-fetched to suggest that the content of a
registered mark is government speech. If the federal registration of a
trademark makes the mark government speech, the Federal Government

is babbling prodigiously and incoherently. It is saying many unseemly things. It is expressing contradictory views. It is unashamedly endorsing a vast array of commercial products and services.

None of our government speech cases even remotely supports the idea that registered trademarks are government speech.

[T]rademarks often have an expressive content. Companies spend huge amounts to create and publicize trademarks that convey a message. It is true that the necessary brevity of trademarks limits what they can say. But powerful messages can sometimes be conveyed in just a few words. Trademarks are private, not government, speech.

B

We next address the Government's argument that this case is governed by cases in which this Court has upheld the constitutionality of government programs that subsidized speech expressing a particular viewpoint. These cases implicate a notoriously tricky question of constitutional law. "[W]e have held that the Government 'may not deny a benefit to a person on a basis that infringes his constitutionally protected . . . freedom of speech even if he has no entitlement to that benefit.'" But at the same time, government is not required to subsidize activities that it does not wish to promote. Determining which of these principles applies in a particular case "is not always self-evident," but no difficult question is presented here.

Unlike the present case, the decisions on which the Government relies all involved cash subsidies or their equivalent. The federal registration of a trademark is nothing like the programs at issue in these cases. The PTO does not pay money to parties seeking registration of a mark. Quite the contrary is true: An applicant for registration must pay the PTO a filing fee of $225–$600. And to maintain federal registration, the holder of a mark must pay a fee of $300–$500 every 10 years.

The Government responds that registration provides valuable nonmonetary benefits that "are directly traceable to the resources devoted by the federal government to examining, publishing, and issuing certificates of registration for those marks." But just about every government service requires the expenditure of government funds. This is true of services that benefit everyone, like police and fire protection, as well as services that are utilized by only some, *e.g.*, the adjudication of private lawsuits and the use of public parks and highways.

Trademark registration is not the only government registration scheme. For example, the Federal Government registers copyrights and patents.

State governments and their subdivisions register the title to real property and security interests; they issue driver's licenses, motor vehicle registrations, and hunting, fishing, and boating licenses or permits.

C

Finally, the Government urges us to sustain the disparagement clause under a new doctrine that would apply to "government-program" cases. For the most part, this argument simply merges our government-speech cases and the previously discussed subsidy cases in an attempt to construct a broader doctrine that can be applied to the registration of trademarks. The only new element in this construct consists of two cases involving a public employer's collection of union dues from its employees. But those cases occupy a special area of First Amendment case law, and they are far removed from the registration of trademarks.

Potentially more analogous are cases in which a unit of government creates a limited public forum for private speech. When government creates such a forum, in either a literal or "metaphysical" sense, some content- and speaker-based restrictions may be allowed. However, even in such cases, what we have termed "viewpoint discrimination" is forbidden.

Our cases use the term "viewpoint" discrimination in a broad sense, and in that sense, the disparagement clause discriminates on the bases of "viewpoint." To be sure, the clause evenhandedly prohibits disparagement of all groups. It applies equally to marks that damn Democrats and Republicans, capitalists and socialists, and those arrayed on both sides of every possible issue. It denies registration to any mark that is offensive to a substantial percentage of the members of any group. But in the sense relevant here, that is viewpoint discrimination: Giving offense is a viewpoint.

We have said time and again that "the public expression of ideas may not be prohibited merely because the ideas are themselves offensive to some of their hearers." For this reason, the disparagement clause cannot be saved by analyzing it as a type of government program in which some content- and speaker-based restrictions are permitted.

IV

Having concluded that the disparagement clause cannot be sustained under our government-speech or subsidy cases or under the Government's proposed "government-program" doctrine, we must confront a dispute between the parties on the question whether trademarks are commercial speech and are thus subject to the relaxed scrutiny outlined in *Central Hudson Gas & Elec. Corp. v. Public Serv. Comm'n of N. Y.* (1980). The Government and *amici* supporting its position argue that all trademarks are commercial speech. They note that the central purposes of trademarks are commercial and that federal law regulates trademarks to promote fair and orderly interstate commerce. Tam and his *amici,* on the other hand, contend that many, if not all, trademarks have an expressive component. In other words, these trademarks do not simply identify the source of a product or service but go on to say something more, either about the product or service or some broader issue. The trademark in this case illustrates this point. The name "The Slants" not only identifies the band but expresses a view about social issues.

We need not resolve this debate between the parties because the disparagement clause cannot withstand even *Central Hudson* review. Under *Central Hudson,* a restriction of speech must serve "a substantial interest," and it must be "narrowly drawn." This means, among other things, that "[t]he regulatory technique may extend only as far as the interest it serves." The disparagement clause fails this requirement.

It is claimed that the disparagement clause serves two interests. The first is phrased in a variety of ways in the briefs. Echoing language in one of the opinions below, the Government asserts an interest in preventing "underrepresented groups" from being "bombarded with demeaning messages in commercial advertising.'" But no matter how the point is phrased, its unmistakable thrust is this: The Government has an interest in preventing speech expressing ideas that offend. And, as we have explained, that idea strikes at the heart of the First Amendment. Speech that demeans on the basis of race, ethnicity, gender, religion, age, disability, or any other similar ground is hateful; but the proudest boast of our free speech jurisprudence is that we protect the freedom to express "the thought that we hate." *United States v. Schwimmer* (1929) (Holmes, J., dissenting).

The second interest asserted is protecting the orderly flow of commerce. Commerce, we are told, is disrupted by trademarks that "involv[e] disparagement of race, gender, ethnicity, national origin, religion, sexual orientation, and similar demographic classification." A simple answer to this argument is that the disparagement clause is not "narrowly drawn" to drive out trademarks that support invidious discrimination. The clause reaches any trademark that disparages *any person, group, or institution*. It applies to trademarks like the following: "Down with racists," "Down with sexists," "Down with homophobes." It is not an anti-discrimination clause; it is a happy-talk clause. In this way, it goes much further than is necessary to serve the interest asserted.

The clause is far too broad in other ways as well. The clause protects every person living or dead as well as every institution. Is it conceivable that commerce would be disrupted by a trademark saying: "James Buchanan was a disastrous president" or "Slavery is an evil institution"?

There is also a deeper problem with the argument that commercial speech may be cleansed of any expression likely to cause offense. The commercial market is well stocked with merchandise that disparages prominent figures and groups, and the line between commercial and noncommercial speech is not always clear, as this case illustrates. If affixing the commercial label permits the suppression of any speech that may lead to political or social "volatility," free speech would be endangered.

For these reasons, we hold that the disparagement clause violates the Free Speech Clause of the First Amendment.

Justice KENNEDY, with whom Justice GINSBURG, Justice SOTOMAYOR, and Justice KAGAN join, concurring in part and concurring in the judgment.

As the Court is correct to hold, § 1052(a) constitutes viewpoint discrimination — a form of speech suppression so potent that it must be subject to rigorous constitutional scrutiny. The Government's action and the statute on which it is based cannot survive this scrutiny.

The Court is correct in its judgment, and I join Parts I, II, and III–A of its opinion. This separate writing explains in greater detail why the First Amendment's protections against viewpoint discrimination apply to the trademark here. It submits further that the viewpoint discrimination rationale renders unnecessary any extended treatment of other questions raised by the parties.

I

Those few categories of speech that the government can regulate or punish — for instance, fraud, defamation, or incitement — are well established within our constitutional tradition. Aside from these and a few other narrow exceptions, it is a fundamental principle of the First Amendment that the government may not punish or suppress speech based on disapproval of the ideas or perspectives the speech conveys.

The First Amendment guards against laws "targeted at specific subject matter," a form of speech suppression known as content based discrimination. This category includes a subtype of laws that go further, aimed at the suppression of "particular views . . . on a subject." . A law found to discriminate based on viewpoint is an "egregious form of content discrimination," which is "presumptively unconstitutional."

At its most basic, the test for viewpoint discrimination is whether — within the relevant subject category — the government has singled out a subset of messages for disfavor based on the views expressed. In the instant case, the disparagement clause the Government now seeks to implement and enforce identifies the relevant subject as "persons, living or dead, institutions, beliefs, or national symbols." Within that category, an applicant may register a positive or benign mark but not a derogatory one. The law thus reflects the Government's disapproval of a subset of messages it finds offensive. This is the essence of viewpoint discrimination.

The Government disputes this conclusion. It argues, to begin with, that the law is viewpoint neutral because it applies in equal measure to any trademark that demeans or offends. This misses the point. A subject that is first defined by content and then regulated or censored by mandating only one sort of comment is not viewpoint neutral. To prohibit all sides from criticizing their opponents makes a law more viewpoint based, not less so. The logic of the Government's rule is that a law would be viewpoint neutral even if it provided that public officials could be praised but not condemned. The First Amendment's viewpoint neutrality principle protects more than the right to identify with a particular side. It protects the right to create and present arguments for particular positions in particular ways, as the speaker chooses. By mandating positivity, the law here might silence dissent and distort the marketplace of ideas.

The Government next suggests that the statute is viewpoint neutral because the disparagement clause applies to trademarks regardless of the applicant's personal views or reasons for using the mark. Instead, registration is denied based on the expected reaction of the applicant's audience. The Government may not insulate a law from charges of viewpoint discrimination by tying censorship to the reaction of the speaker's audience. The Court has suggested that viewpoint discrimination occurs when the government intends to suppress a speaker's beliefs, but viewpoint discrimination need not take that form in every instance. The danger of viewpoint discrimination is that the government is attempting to remove certain ideas or perspectives from a broader debate. That danger is all the greater if the ideas or perspectives are ones a particular audience might think offensive, at least at first hearing. An initial reaction may prompt further reflection, leading to a more reasoned, more tolerant position.

Indeed, a speech burden based on audience reactions is simply government hostility and intervention in a different guise. The speech is targeted, after all, based on the government's disapproval of the speaker's choice of message. And it is the government itself that is attempting in this case to decide whether the relevant audience would find the speech offensive. For reasons like these, the Court's cases have long prohibited the government from justifying a First Amendment burden by pointing to the offensiveness of the speech to be suppressed.

## II

The parties dispute whether trademarks are commercial speech and whether trademark registration should be considered a federal subsidy. The former issue may turn on whether certain commercial concerns for the protection of trademarks might, as a general matter, be the basis for regulation. However that issue is resolved, the viewpoint based discrimination at issue here necessarily invokes heightened scrutiny. "Commercial speech is no exception," the Court has explained, to the principle that the First Amendment "requires heightened scrutiny whenever the government creates a regulation of speech because of disagreement with the message it conveys." Unlike content based discrimination, discrimination based on viewpoint, including a regulation that targets speech for its offensiveness, remains of serious concern in the commercial context.

A law that can be directed against speech found offensive to some portion of the public can be turned against minority and dissenting views to the detriment of all. The First Amendment does not entrust that power to the government's benevolence. Instead, our reliance must be on the substantial safeguards of free and open discussion in a democratic society. For these reasons, I join the Court's opinion in part and concur in the judgment.

## 2.  Vagueness and Overbreadth

### b.  *Overbreadth* (casebook p. 1285)

Although the Court did not explicitly use overbreadth analysis, in *Packingham v. North Carolina*, the Court concluded that a law preventing those convicted of sex crimes from being on social media was too broad and violated the First Amendment. Justice Kennedy's opinion may be particularly important for its discussion of the importance of protecting speech on the internet.

## PACKINGHAM v. NORTH CAROLINA
137 S. Ct. ___ (2018)

Justice KENNEDY delivered the opinion of the Court.

In 2008, North Carolina enacted a statute making it a felony for a registered sex offender to gain access to a number of websites, including commonplace social media websites like Facebook and Twitter. The question presented is whether that law is permissible under the First Amendment's Free Speech Clause, applicable to the States under the Due Process Clause of the Fourteenth Amendment.

I

North Carolina law makes it a felony for a registered sex offender "to access a commercial social networking Web site where the sex offender knows that the site permits minor children to become members or to create or maintain personal Web pages." A "commercial social networking Web site" is defined as a website that meets four criteria. First, it "[i]s operated by a person who derives revenue from membership fees, advertising, or other sources related to the operation of the Website." Second, it "[f]acilitates the social introduction between two or more persons for the purposes of friendship, meeting other persons, or information exchanges." Third, it "[a]llows users to create Web pages or personal profiles that contain information such as the name or nickname of the user, photographs placed on the personal Web page by the user, other personal information about the user, and links to other personal Web pages on the commercial social networking Web site of friends or associates of the user that may be accessed by other users or visitors to the Web site." And fourth, it "[p]rovides users or visitors . . . mechanisms to communicate with other users, such as a message board, chat room, electronic mail, or instant messenger."

The statute includes two express exemptions. The statutory bar does not extend to websites that "[p]rovid[e] only one of the following discrete services: photo-sharing, electronic mail, instant messenger, or chat room or message board platform." The law also does not encompass websites that have as their "primary purpose the facilitation of commercial transactions involving goods or services between [their] members or visitors."

According to sources cited to the Court, § 14–202.5 applies to about 20,000 people in North Carolina and the State has prosecuted over 1,000 people for violating it.

B

In 2002, petitioner Lester Gerard Packingham—then a 21–year–old college student—had sex with a 13–year–old girl. He pleaded guilty to taking indecent liberties with a child. Because this crime qualifies as "an offense against a minor," petitioner was required to register as a sex offender—a status that can endure for 30 years or more. As a registered sex offender, petitioner was barred under § 14–202.5 from gaining access to commercial social networking sites.

In 2010, a state court dismissed a traffic ticket against petitioner. In response, he logged on to Facebook.com and posted the following statement on his personal profile:

"Man God is Good! How about I got so much favor they dismissed the ticket before court even started? No fine, no court cost, no nothing spent . . . . . . Praise be to GOD, WOW! Thanks JESUS!"

At the time, a member of the Durham Police Department was investigating registered sex offenders who were thought to be violating § 14–202.5. The officer noticed that a " 'J.R. Gerrard' " had posted the statement quoted above. 777 S.E.2d 738, 742 (2015). By checking court records, the officer discovered that a traffic citation for petitioner had been dismissed around the time of the post. Evidence obtained by search warrant confirmed the officer's suspicions that petitioner was J.R. Gerrard.

Petitioner was indicted by a grand jury for violating § 14–202.5. The trial court denied his motion to dismiss the indictment on the grounds that the charge against him violated the First Amendment. Petitioner was ultimately convicted and given a suspended prison sentence. At no point during trial or sentencing did the State allege that petitioner contacted a minor—or committed any other illicit act—on the Internet.

II

A fundamental principle of the First Amendment is that all persons have access to places where they can speak and listen, and then, after reflection, speak and listen once more. The Court has sought to protect the right to speak in this spatial context. A basic rule, for example, is that a street or a park is a quintessential forum for the exercise of First Amendment rights. Even in the modern era, these places are still essential venues for public gatherings to celebrate some views, to protest others, or simply to learn and inquire.

While in the past there may have been difficulty in identifying the most important places (in a spatial sense) for the exchange of views, today the answer is clear. It is cyberspace—the "vast democratic forums of the

Internet" in general and social media in particular. Seven in ten American adults use at least one Internet social networking service. One of the most popular of these sites is Facebook, the site used by petitioner leading to his conviction in this case. According to sources cited to the Court in this case, Facebook has 1.79 billion active users. This is about three times the population of North America.

Social media offers "relatively unlimited, low-cost capacity for communication of all kinds." On Facebook, for example, users can debate religion and politics with their friends and neighbors or share vacation photos. On LinkedIn, users can look for work, advertise for employees, or review tips on entrepreneurship. And on Twitter, users can petition their elected representatives and otherwise engage with them in a direct manner. Indeed, Governors in all 50 States and almost every Member of Congress have set up accounts for this purpose. In short, social media users employ these websites to engage in a wide array of protected First Amendment activity on topics "as diverse as human thought."

The nature of a revolution in thought can be that, in its early stages, even its participants may be unaware of it. And when awareness comes, they still may be unable to know or foresee where its changes lead. So too here. While we now may be coming to the realization that the Cyber Age is a revolution of historic proportions, we cannot appreciate yet its full dimensions and vast potential to alter how we think, express ourselves, and define who we want to be. The forces and directions of the Internet are so new, so protean, and so far reaching that courts must be conscious that what they say today might be obsolete tomorrow.

This case is one of the first this Court has taken to address the relationship between the First Amendment and the modern Internet. As a result, the Court must exercise extreme caution before suggesting that the First Amendment provides scant protection for access to vast networks in that medium.

III

This background informs the analysis of the North Carolina statute at issue. Even making the assumption that the statute is content neutral and thus subject to intermediate scrutiny, the provision cannot stand. In order to survive intermediate scrutiny, a law must be "narrowly tailored to serve a significant governmental interest."

For centuries now, inventions heralded as advances in human progress have been exploited by the criminal mind. New technologies, all too soon, can become instruments used to commit serious crimes. The railroad is one example, and the telephone another. So it will be with the Internet and social media.

There is also no doubt that, as this Court has recognized, "[t]he sexual abuse of a child is a most serious crime and an act repugnant to the moral instincts of a decent people." And it is clear that a legislature "may pass valid laws to protect children" and other victims of sexual assault "from abuse." The government, of course, need not simply stand by and allow these evils to occur. But the assertion of a valid governmental interest "cannot, in every context, be insulated from all constitutional protections."

It is necessary to make two assumptions to resolve this case. First, given the broad wording of the North Carolina statute at issue, it might well bar access not only to commonplace social media websites but also to websites as varied as Amazon.com, Washingtonpost.com, and Webmd. com. The Court need not decide the precise scope of the statute. It is enough to assume that the law applies (as the State concedes it does) to social networking sites "as commonly understood" — that is, websites like Facebook, LinkedIn, and Twitter.

Second, this opinion should not be interpreted as barring a State from enacting more specific laws than the one at issue. Specific criminal acts are not protected speech even if speech is the means for their commission. Though the issue is not before the Court, it can be assumed that the First Amendment permits a State to enact specific, narrowly tailored laws that prohibit a sex offender from engaging in conduct that often presages a sexual crime, like contacting a minor or using a website to gather information about a minor. Specific laws of that type must be the State's first resort to ward off the serious harm that sexual crimes inflict. (Of importance, the troubling fact that the law imposes severe restrictions on persons who already have served their sentence and are no longer subject to the supervision of the criminal justice system is also not an issue before the Court.)

Even with these assumptions about the scope of the law and the State's interest, the statute here enacts a prohibition unprecedented in the scope of First Amendment speech it burdens. Social media allows users to gain access to information and communicate with one another about it on any subject that might come to mind. By prohibiting sex offenders from using those websites, North Carolina with one broad stroke bars access to what for many are the principal sources for knowing current events, checking ads for employment, speaking and listening in the modern public square, and otherwise exploring the vast realms of human thought and knowledge. These websites can provide perhaps the most powerful mechanisms available to a private citizen to make his or her voice heard. They allow a person with an Internet connection to "become a town crier with a voice that resonates farther than it could from any soapbox."

In sum, to foreclose access to social media altogether is to prevent the user from engaging in the legitimate exercise of First Amendment rights. It is unsettling to suggest that only a limited set of websites can be used even by persons who have completed their sentences. Even convicted criminals — and in some instances especially convicted criminals — might receive legitimate benefits from these means for access to the world of ideas, in particular if they seek to reform and to pursue lawful and rewarding lives.

## IV

The primary response from the State is that the law must be this broad to serve its preventative purpose of keeping convicted sex offenders away from vulnerable victims. The State has not, however, met its burden to show that this sweeping law is necessary or legitimate to serve that purpose. It is instructive that no case or holding of this Court has approved of a statute as broad in its reach.

It is well established that, as a general rule, the Government "may not suppress lawful speech as the means to suppress unlawful speech." That is what North Carolina has done here. Its law must be held invalid.

Justice ALITO, with whom THE CHIEF JUSTICE and Justice THOMAS join, concurring in the judgment.

The North Carolina statute at issue in this case was enacted to serve an interest of "surpassing importance" — but it has a staggering reach. It makes it a felony for a registered sex offender simply to visit a vast array of websites, including many that appear to provide no realistic opportunity for communications that could facilitate the abuse of children. Because of the law's extraordinary breadth, I agree with the Court that it violates the Free Speech Clause of the First Amendment.

I cannot join the opinion of the Court, however, because of its undisciplined dicta. The Court is unable to resist musings that seem to equate the entirety of the internet with public streets and parks. And this language is bound to be interpreted by some to mean that the States are largely powerless to restrict even the most dangerous sexual predators from visiting any internet sites, including, for example, teenage dating sites and sites designed to permit minors to discuss personal problems with their peers. I am troubled by the implications of the Court's unnecessary rhetoric.

I

As we have frequently noted, "[t]he prevention of sexual exploitation and abuse of children constitutes a government objective of surpassing importance." "Sex offenders are a serious threat," and "the victims of sexual assault are most often juveniles." "[T]he . . . interest [of] safeguarding the physical and psychological well-being of a minor . . . is a compelling one," and "we have sustained legislation aimed at protecting the physical and emotional well-being of youth even when the laws have operated in the sensitive area of constitutionally protected rights." Repeat sex offenders pose an especially grave risk to children. "When convicted sex offenders reenter society, they are much more likely than any other type of offender to be rearrested for a new rape or sexual assault."

The State's interest in protecting children from recidivist sex offenders plainly applies to internet use. Several factors make the internet a powerful tool for the would-be child abuser. First, children often use the internet in a way that gives offenders easy access to their personal information — by, for example, communicating with strangers and allowing sites to disclose their location. Second, the internet provides previously unavailable ways of communicating with, stalking, and ultimately abusing children. An abuser can create a false profile that misrepresents the abuser's age and gender. The abuser can lure the minor into engaging in sexual conversations, sending explicit photos, or even meeting in person. And an abuser can use a child's location posts on the internet to determine the pattern of the child's day-to-day activities — and even the child's location at a given moment. Such uses of the internet are already well documented, both in research and in reported decisions.

Because protecting children from abuse is a compelling state interest and sex offenders can (and do) use the internet to engage in such abuse, it is legitimate and entirely reasonable for States to try to stop abuse from occurring before it happens.

It is not enough, however, that the law before us is designed to serve a compelling state interest; it also must not "burden substantially more speech than is necessary to further the government's legitimate interests." The North Carolina law fails this requirement.

A straightforward reading of the text of N.C. Gen. Stat. Ann. § 14–202.5 compels the conclusion that it prohibits sex offenders from accessing an enormous number of websites.

The fatal problem for § 14–202.5 is that its wide sweep precludes access to a large number of websites that are most unlikely to facilitate the commission of a sex crime against a child. A handful of examples illustrates this point. Take, for example, the popular retail website Amazon.com, which allows minors to use its services and meets all four requirements of § 14–202.5's definition of a commercial social networking website. Many news websites are also covered by this definition. For example, the Washington Post's website gives minors access and satisfies the four elements that define a commercial social networking website. Or consider WebMD—a website that contains health-related resources, from tools that help users find a doctor to information on preventative care and the symptoms associated with particular medical problems. WebMD, too, allows children on the site. And it exhibits the four hallmarks of a "commercial social networking" website.

As these examples illustrate, the North Carolina law has a very broad reach and covers websites that are ill suited for use in stalking or abusing children. The focus of the discussion on these sites—shopping, news, health—does not provide a convenient jumping off point for conversations that may lead to abuse. In addition, the social exchanges facilitated by these websites occur in the open, and this reduces the possibility of a child being secretly lured into an abusive situation. These websites also give sex offenders little opportunity to gather personal details about a child; the information that can be listed in a profile is limited, and the profiles are brief. What is more, none of these websites make it easy to determine a child's precise location at a given moment. For example, they do not permit photo streams (at most, a child could upload a single profile photograph), and they do not include up-to-the minute location services. Such websites would provide essentially no aid to a would-be child abuser.

Placing this set of websites categorically off limits from registered sex offenders prohibits them from receiving or engaging in speech that the First Amendment protects and does not appreciably advance the State's goal of protecting children from recidivist sex offenders. I am therefore compelled to conclude that, while the law before us addresses a critical problem, it sweeps far too broadly to satisfy the demands of the Free Speech Clause.

## II

While I thus agree with the Court that the particular law at issue in this case violates the First Amendment, I am troubled by the Court's loose rhetoric. After noting that "a street or a park is a quintessential forum for the exercise of First Amendment rights," the Court states that "cyberspace" and "social media in particular" are now "the most important places (in a spatial sense) for the exchange of views." But if the entirety of the internet or even just "social media" sites[16] are the 21st century equivalent of public streets and parks, then States may have little ability to restrict the sites that may be visited by even the most dangerous sex offenders. May a State preclude an adult previously convicted of molesting children from visiting a dating site for teenagers? Or a site where minors communicate with each other about personal problems? The Court should be more attentive to the implications of its rhetoric for, contrary to the Court's suggestion, there are important differences between cyberspace and the physical world.

I will mention a few that are relevant to internet use by sex offenders. First, it is easier for parents to monitor the physical locations that their children visit and the individuals with whom they speak in person than it is to monitor their internet use. Second, if a sex offender is seen approaching children or loitering in a place frequented by children, this conduct may be observed by parents, teachers, or others. Third, the internet offers an unprecedented degree of anonymity and easily permits a would-be molester to assume a false identity.

The Court is correct that we should be cautious in applying our free speech precedents to the internet. Cyberspace is different from the physical world, and if it is true, as the Court believes, that "we cannot appreciate yet" the "full dimensions and vast potential" of "the Cyber Age," we should proceed circumspectly, taking one step at a time. It is regrettable that the Court has not heeded its own admonition of caution.


## 5. Commercial speech

### b.  What is Commercial Speech? (p. 1478)

As *Sorrell v. IMS Health Care* (p. 1480) shows, the issue often arises as to when regulation of commercial transactions should be regarded as a regulation of commercial speech. That is the issue in *Expressions Hair Design v. Schneiderman*.


EXPRESSIONS HAIR DESIGN v. SCHNEIDERMAN
137 S. Ct. 1144 (2017)

Chief Justice ROBERTS delivered the opinion of the Court.

Each time a customer pays for an item with a credit card, the merchant selling that item must pay a transaction fee to the credit card issuer.

Some merchants balk at paying the fees and want to discourage the use of credit cards, or at least pass on the fees to customers who use them. One method of achieving those ends is through differential pricing — charging credit card users more than customers using cash. Merchants who wish to employ differential pricing may do so in two ways relevant here: impose a surcharge for the use of a credit card, or offer a discount for the use of cash. In N.Y. Gen. Bus. Law § 518, New York has banned the former practice. The question presented is whether § 518 regulates merchants' speech and — if so — whether the statute violates the First Amendment. We conclude that § 518does regulate speech and remand for the Court of Appeals to determine in the first instance whether that regulation is unconstitutional.

I

When credit cards were first introduced, contracts between card issuers and merchants barred merchants from charging credit card users higher prices than cash customers. Congress put a partial stop to this practice in the 1974 amendments to the Truth in Lending Act (TILA). The amendments prohibited card issuers from contractually preventing merchants from giving discounts to customers who paid in cash. The law, however, said nothing about surcharges for the use of credit.

Two years later, Congress refined its dissimilar treatment of discounts and surcharges. First, the 1976 version of TILA barred merchants from imposing surcharges on customers who use credit cards. Second, Congress added definitions of the two terms. A discount was "a reduction made from the regular price," while a surcharge was "any means of increasing the regular price to a cardholder which is not imposed upon customers paying by cash, check, or similar means."

In 1981, Congress further delineated the distinction between discounts and surcharges by defining "regular price." Where a merchant "tagged or posted" a single price, the regular price was that single price. If no price was tagged or posted, or if a merchant employed a two-tag approach — posting one price for credit and another for cash — the regular price was whatever was charged to credit card users. Because a surcharge was defined as an increase from the regular price, there could be no credit card surcharge where the regular price was the same as the amount charged to customers using credit cards. The effect of all this was that a merchant could violate the surcharge ban only by posting a single price and charging credit card users more than that posted price.

The federal surcharge ban was short lived. Congress allowed it to expire in 1984 and has not renewed the ban since. The provision preventing credit card issuers from contractually barring discounts for cash, however, remained in place. With the lapse of the federal surcharge ban, several States, New York among them, immediately enacted their own surcharge bans. Passed in 1984, N.Y. Gen. Bus. Law § 518 adopted the operative language of the federal ban verbatim, providing that "[n]o seller in any sales transaction may impose a surcharge on a holder who elects to use a credit card in lieu of payment by cash, check, or similar means." Unlike the federal ban, the New York legislation included no definition of "surcharge."

In addition to these state legislative bans, credit card companies—though barred from prohibiting discounts for cash—included provisions in their contracts prohibiting merchants from imposing surcharges for credit card use. For most of its history, the New York law was essentially coextensive with these contractual prohibitions. In recent years, however, merchants have brought antitrust challenges to contractual no-surcharge provisions. Those suits have created uncertainty about the legal validity of such contractual surcharge bans. The result is that otherwise redundant legislative surcharge bans like § 518 have increasingly gained importance, and increasingly come under scrutiny.

Petitioners, five New York businesses and their owners, wish to impose surcharges on customers who use credit cards. Each time one of their customers pays with a credit card, these merchants must pay some transaction fee to the company that issued the credit card. The fee is generally two to three percent of the purchase price. Those fees add up, and the merchants allege that they pay tens of thousands of dollars every year to credit card companies. Rather than increase prices across the board to absorb those costs, the merchants want to pass the fees along only to their customers who choose to use credit cards. They also want to make clear that they are not the bad guys—that the credit card companies, not the merchants, are responsible for the higher prices. The merchants believe that surcharges for credit are more effective than discounts for cash in accomplishing these goals.

In 2013, after several major credit card issuers agreed to drop their contractual surcharge prohibitions, the merchants filed suit against the New York Attorney General and three New York District Attorneys to challenge § 518—the only remaining obstacle to their charging surcharges for credit card use. As relevant here, they argued that the law violated the First Amendment by regulating how they communicated their prices, and that it was unconstitutionally vague because liability under the law "turn[ed] on the blurry difference" between surcharges and discounts.

The District Court ruled in favor of the merchants. It read the statute as "draw[ing a] line between prohibited 'surcharges' and permissible 'discounts' based on words and labels, rather than economic realities." The court concluded that the law therefore regulated speech, and violated the First Amendment under this Court's commercial speech doctrine. In addition, because the law turned on the "virtually incomprehensible distinction between what a vendor can and cannot tell its customers," the District Court found that the law was unconstitutionally vague.

The Court of Appeals for the Second Circuit vacated the judgment of the District Court with instructions to dismiss the merchants' claims. It began by considering single-sticker pricing, where merchants post one price and would like to charge more to customers who pay by credit card. All the law did in this context, the Court of Appeals explained, was regulate a relationship between two prices—the sticker price and the price charged to a credit card user—by requiring that the two prices be equal. Relying on our precedent holding that price regulation alone regulates conduct, not speech, the Court of Appeals concluded that § 518 did not violate the First Amendment.

## II

As a preliminary matter, we note that petitioners present us with a limited challenge. Observing that the merchants were not always particularly clear about the scope of their suit, the Court of Appeals deemed them to be bringing a facial attack on § 518 as well as a challenge to the application of the statute to two particular pricing regimes: single-sticker pricing and two-sticker pricing. Before us, however, the merchants have disclaimed a facial challenge, assuring us that theirs is an as-applied challenge only.

There remains the question of what precise application of the law they seek to challenge. Although the merchants have presented a wide array of hypothetical pricing regimes, they have expressly identified only one pricing scheme that they seek to employ: posting a cash price and an additional credit card surcharge, expressed either as a percentage surcharge or a "dollars-and-cents" additional amount. Under this pricing approach, petitioner Expressions Hair Design might, for example, post a sign outside its salon reading "Haircuts $10 (we add a 3% surcharge if you pay by credit card)." Or, petitioner Brooklyn Farmacy & Soda Fountain might list one of the sundaes on its menu as costing "$10 (with a $0.30 surcharge for credit card users)." We take petitioners at their word and limit our review to the question whether § 518 is unconstitutional as applied to this particular pricing practice.

## III

The next question is whether § 518 prohibits the pricing regime petitioners wish to employ. The Court of Appeals concluded that it does. The court read "surcharge" in § 518 to mean "an additional amount above the seller's regular price," and found it "basically self-evident" how § 518 applies to sellers who post a single sticker price: "the sticker price is the 'regular' price, so sellers may not charge credit-card customers an additional amount above the sticker price that is not also charged to cash customers." Under this interpretation, signs of the kind that the merchants wish to post — "$10, with a $0.30 surcharge for credit card users" — violate § 518 because they identify one sticker price — $10 — and indicate that credit card users are charged more than that amount.

"We generally accord great deference to the interpretation and application of state law by the courts of appeals." This deference is warranted to "render unnecessary review of their decisions in this respect" and because lower federal courts "are better schooled in and more able to interpret the laws of their respective States." "[W]e surely have the authority to differ with the lower federal courts as to the meaning of a state statute," and have done so in instances where the lower court's construction was "clearly wrong" or "plain error." But that is not the case here. Section 518 does not define "surcharge," but the Court of Appeals looked to the ordinary meaning of the term: "a charge in excess of the usual or normal amount." Where a seller posts a single sticker price, it is reasonable to treat that sticker price as the "usual or normal amount" and conclude, as the court below did, that a merchant imposes a surcharge when he charges a credit card user more than that sticker price. In short, we cannot dismiss the Court of Appeals' interpretation of § 518 as "clearly wrong." Accordingly, consistent with our customary practice, we follow that interpretation.

## IV

Having concluded that § 518 bars the pricing regime petitioners wish to employ, we turn to their constitutional arguments: that the law unconstitutionally regulates speech and is impermissibly vague.

The Court of Appeals concluded that § 518 posed no First Amendment problem because the law regulated conduct, not speech. In reaching this conclusion, the Court of Appeals began with the premise that price controls regulate conduct alone. Section 518 regulates the relationship between "(1) the seller's sticker price and (2) the price the seller charges to credit card customers," requiring that these two amounts be equal. 808 F.3d, at 131. A law regulating the relationship between two prices regulates speech no more than a law regulating a single price. The Court of Appeals concluded that § 518 was therefore simply a conduct regulation.

But §518 is not like a typical price regulation. Such a regulation — for example, a law requiring all New York delis to charge $10 for their sandwiches — would simply regulate the amount that a store could collect. In other words, it would regulate the sandwich seller's conduct. To be sure, in order to actually collect that money, a store would likely have to put "$10" on its menus or have its employees tell customers that price. Those written or oral communications would be speech, and the law — by determining the amount charged — would indirectly dictate the content of that speech. But the law's effect on speech would be only incidental to its primary effect on conduct, and "it has never been deemed an abridgment of freedom of speech or press to make a course of conduct illegal merely because the conduct was in part initiated, evidenced, or carried out by means of language, either spoken, written, or printed."

Section 518 is different. The law tells merchants nothing about the amount they are allowed to collect from a cash or credit card payer. Sellers are free to charge $10 for cash and $9.70, $10, $10.30, or any other amount for credit. What the law does regulate is how sellers may communicate their prices. A merchant who wants to charge $10 for cash and $10.30 for credit may not convey that price any way he pleases. He is not free to say "$10, with a 3% credit card surcharge" or "$10, plus $0.30 for credit" because both of those displays identify a single sticker price — $10 — that is less than the amount credit card users will be charged. Instead, if the merchant wishes to post a single sticker price, he must display $10.30 as his sticker price. Accordingly, while we agree with the Court of Appeals that § 518 regulates a relationship between a sticker price and the price charged to credit card users, we cannot accept its conclusion that § 518 is nothing more than a mine-run price regulation. In regulating the communication of prices rather than prices themselves, § 518 regulates speech.

Because it concluded otherwise, the Court of Appeals had no occasion to conduct a further inquiry into whether § 518, as a speech regulation, survived First Amendment scrutiny. On that question, the parties dispute whether § 518 is a valid commercial speech regulation under *Central Hudson Gas & Elec. Corp. v. Public Serv. Comm'n of N.Y.* (1980), and

whether the law can be upheld as a valid disclosure requirement. "[W]
e are a court of review, not of first view." Accordingly, we decline to
consider those questions in the first instance. Instead, we remand for the
Court of Appeals to analyze § 518 as a speech regulation.[3]

Justice BREYER, concurring in the judgment.
I agree with the Court that New York's statute regulates speech. But
that is because virtually all government regulation affects speech. Human
relations take place through speech. And human relations include community activities of all kinds — commercial and otherwise.
When the government seeks to regulate those activities, it is often wiser
not to try to distinguish between "speech" and "conduct." Instead, we
can, and normally do, simply ask whether, or how, a challenged statute,
rule, or regulation affects an interest that the First Amendment protects.
If, for example, a challenged government regulation negatively affects the
processes through which political discourse or public opinion is formed
or expressed (interests close to the First Amendment's protective core),
courts normally scrutinize that regulation with great care.
If the challenged regulation restricts the "informational function" provided by truthful commercial speech, courts will apply a "lesser" (but
still elevated) form of scrutiny. If, however, a challenged regulation simply requires a commercial speaker to disclose "purely factual and uncon-
troversial information," courts will apply a more permissive standard of
review. Because that kind of regulation normally has only a "minimal"
effect on First Amendment interests, it normally need only be "reasonably related to the State's interest in preventing deception of consumers."
Courts apply a similarly permissive standard of review to "regulatory
legislation affecting ordinary commercial transactions." *United States v.
Carolene Products Co.* (1938). Since that legislation normally does not
significantly affect the interests that the First Amendment protects, we
normally look only for assurance that the legislation "rests upon some
rational basis."
I repeat these well-known general standards or judicial approaches
both because I believe that determining the proper approach is typically
more important than trying to distinguish "speech" from "conduct,"
and because the parties here differ as to which approach applies. That
difference reflects the fact that it is not clear just what New York's law
does. On its face, the law seems simply to tell merchants that they cannot charge higher prices to credit-card users. If so, then it is an ordinary
piece of commercial legislation subject to "rational basis" review. It may,
however, make more sense to interpret the statute as working like the

expired federal law that it replaced. If so, it would require a merchant, who posts prices and who wants to charge a higher credit-card price, simply to disclose that credit-card price. In that case, though affecting the merchant's "speech," it would not hinder the transmission of information to the public; the merchant would remain free to say whatever it wanted so long as it also revealed its credit-card price to customers. Accordingly, the law would still receive a deferential form of review.

Nonetheless, petitioners suggest that the statute does more. Because the statute's operation is unclear and because its interpretation is a matter of state law, I agree with the majority that we should remand the case to the Second Circuit. I also agree with Justice Sotomayor that on remand, it may well be helpful for the Second Circuit to ask the New York Court of Appeals to clarify the nature of the obligations the statute imposes.

Justice Sotomayor, with whom Justice Alito joins, concurring in the judgment.

The Court addresses only one part of one half of petitioners' First Amendment challenge to the New York statute at issue here. This quarter-loaf outcome is worse than none. I would vacate the judgment below and remand with directions to certify the case to the New York Court of Appeals for a definitive interpretation of the statute that would permit the full resolution of petitioners' claims.

# Chapter 10

## The First Amendment: Religion

### B. The Free Exercise Clause

### 3. Is Denial of Funding for Religious Education a Violation of Free Exercise of Religion? (casebook p. 1756)

TRINITY LUTHERAN CHURCH OF COLUMBIA,
MISSOURI v. PAULEY
137 S. Ct. ___ (2017)

Chief Justice ROBERTS delivered the opinion of the Court, except as to footnote 3.

The Missouri Department of Natural Resources offers state grants to help public and private schools, nonprofit daycare centers, and other non-profit entities purchase rubber playground surfaces made from recycled tires. Trinity Lutheran Church applied for such a grant for its preschool and daycare center and would have received one, but for the fact that Trinity Lutheran is a church. The Department had a policy of categorically disqualifying churches and other religious organizations from receiving grants under its playground resurfacing program. The question presented is whether the Department's policy violated the rights of Trinity Lutheran under the Free Exercise Clause of the First Amendment.

I

A

The Trinity Lutheran Church Child Learning Center is a preschool and daycare center open throughout the year to serve working families in Boone County, Missouri, and the surrounding area. Established as a nonprofit organization in 1980, the Center merged with Trinity Lutheran Church in 1985 and operates under its auspices on church property. The

Center admits students of any religion, and enrollment stands at about 90 children ranging from age two to five.

The Center includes a playground that is equipped with the basic playground essentials: slides, swings, jungle gyms, monkey bars, and sandboxes. Almost the entire surface beneath and surrounding the play equipment is coarse pea gravel. Youngsters, of course, often fall on the playground or tumble from the equipment. And when they do, the gravel can be unforgiving.

In 2012, the Center sought to replace a large portion of the pea gravel with a pour-in-place rubber surface by participating in Missouri's Scrap Tire Program. Run by the State's Department of Natural Resources to reduce the number of used tires destined for landfills and dump sites, the program offers reimbursement grants to qualifying nonprofit organizations that purchase playground surfaces made from recycled tires. It is funded through a fee imposed on the sale of new tires in the State.

Due to limited resources, the Department cannot offer grants to all applicants and so awards them on a competitive basis to those scoring highest based on several criteria, such as the poverty level of the population in the surrounding area and the applicant's plan to promote recycling. When the Center applied, the Department had a strict and express policy of denying grants to any applicant owned or controlled by a church, sect, or other religious entity. That policy, in the Department's view, was compelled by Article I, Section 7 of the Missouri Constitution, which provides: "That no money shall ever be taken from the public treasury, directly or indirectly, in aid of any church, sect or denomination of religion, or in aid of any priest, preacher, minister or teacher thereof, as such; and that no preference shall be given to nor any discrimination made against any church, sect or creed of religion, or any form of religious faith or worship."

The Center ranked fifth among the 44 applicants in the 2012 Scrap Tire Program. But despite its high score, the Center was deemed categorically ineligible to receive a grant. In a letter rejecting the Center's application, the program director explained that, under Article I, Section 7 of the Missouri Constitution, the Department could not provide financial assistance directly to a church.

The Department ultimately awarded 14 grants as part of the 2012 program. Because the Center was operated by Trinity Lutheran Church, it did not receive a grant.

B

Trinity Lutheran sued the Director of the Department in Federal District Court. The Church alleged that the Department's failure to approve the Center's application, pursuant to its policy of denying grants to religiously affiliated applicants, violates the Free Exercise Clause of the First Amendment. Trinity Lutheran sought declaratory and injunctive relief prohibiting the Department from discriminating against the Church on that basis in future grant applications.

The District Court granted the Department's motion to dismiss. The Free Exercise Clause, the District Court stated, prohibits the government from outlawing or restricting the exercise of a religious practice; it generally does not prohibit withholding an affirmative benefit on account of religion. The District Court likened the Department's denial of the scrap tire grant to the situation this Court encountered in *Locke v. Davey* (2004). In that case, we upheld against a free exercise challenge the State of Washington's decision not to fund degrees in devotional theology as part of a state scholarship program. Finding the present case "nearly indistinguishable from *Locke,*" the District Court held that the Free Exercise Clause did not require the State to make funds available under the Scrap Tire Program to religious institutions like Trinity Lutheran. The Court of Appeals for the Eighth Circuit affirmed.

## II

The First Amendment provides, in part, that "Congress shall make no law respecting an establishment of religion, or prohibiting the free exercise thereof." The parties agree that the Establishment Clause of that Amendment does not prevent Missouri from including Trinity Lutheran in the Scrap Tire Program. That does not, however, answer the question under the Free Exercise Clause, because we have recognized that there is "play in the joints" between what the Establishment Clause permits and the Free Exercise Clause compels.

The Free Exercise Clause "protect[s] religious observers against unequal treatment" and subjects to the strictest scrutiny laws that target the religious for "special disabilities" based on their "religious status." Applying that basic principle, this Court has repeatedly confirmed that denying a generally available benefit solely on account of religious identity imposes a penalty on the free exercise of religion that can be justified only by a state interest "of the highest order."

In *Everson v. Board of Education of Ewing,* 330 U.S. 1, 67 S. Ct. 504, 91 L. Ed. 711 (1947), for example, we upheld against an Establishment Clause challenge a New Jersey law enabling a local school district to reimburse parents for the public transportation costs of sending their children to public and private schools, including parochial schools. In the course of ruling that the Establishment Clause allowed New Jersey to extend that public benefit to all its citizens regardless of their religious belief, we explained that a State "cannot hamper its citizens in the free exercise of their own religion. Consequently, it cannot exclude individual Catholics, Lutherans, Mohammedans, Baptists, Jews, Methodists, Non-believers, Presbyterians, or the members of any other faith, *because of their faith, or lack of it,* from receiving the benefits of public welfare legislation."

### III

#### A

The Department's policy expressly discriminates against otherwise eligible recipients by disqualifying them from a public benefit solely because of their religious character. If the cases just described make one thing clear, it is that such a policy imposes a penalty on the free exercise of religion that triggers the most exacting scrutiny. This conclusion is unremarkable in light of our prior decisions.

The Department contends that merely declining to extend funds to Trinity Lutheran does not *prohibit* the Church from engaging in any religious conduct or otherwise exercising its religious rights. Here the Department has simply declined to allocate to Trinity Lutheran a subsidy the State had no obligation to provide in the first place. That decision does not meaningfully burden the Church's free exercise rights. And absent any such burden, the argument continues, the Department is free to heed the State's antiestablishment objection to providing funds directly to a church.

It is true the Department has not criminalized the way Trinity Lutheran worships or told the Church that it cannot subscribe to a certain view of the Gospel. But, as the Department itself acknowledges, the Free Exercise Clause protects against "indirect coercion or penalties on the free exercise of religion, not just outright prohibitions." As the Court put it more than 50 years ago, "[i]t is too late in the day to doubt that the liberties of religion and expression may be infringed by the denial of or placing of conditions upon a benefit or privilege."

Trinity Lutheran is not claiming any entitlement to a subsidy. It instead asserts a right to participate in a government benefit program without having to disavow its religious character. The "imposition of such a condition upon even a gratuitous benefit inevitably deter[s] or discourage[s] the exercise of First Amendment rights." The express discrimination against religious exercise here is not the denial of a

grant, but rather the refusal to allow the Church — solely because it is
a church — to compete with secular organizations for a grant. Trinity
Lutheran is a member of the community too, and the State's decision
to exclude it for purposes of this public program must withstand the
strictest scrutiny.

B

The Department attempts to get out from under the weight of our precedents by arguing that the free exercise question in this case is instead
controlled by our decision in *Locke v. Davey.* It is not. In *Locke,* the State
of Washington created a scholarship program to assist high-achieving students with the costs of postsecondary education. The scholarships were
paid out of the State's general fund, and eligibility was based on criteria
such as an applicant's score on college admission tests and family income.
While scholarship recipients were free to use the money at accredited religious and non-religious schools alike, they were not permitted to use the
funds to pursue a devotional theology degree — one "devotional in nature
or designed to induce religious faith." Davey was selected for a scholarship but was denied the funds when he refused to certify that he would
not use them toward a devotional degree. He sued, arguing that the State's
refusal to allow its scholarship money to go toward such degrees violated
his free exercise rights.

At the outset the Court made clear that *Locke* was not like the case now
before us.

Washington's restriction on the use of its scholarship funds was different. According to the Court, the State had "merely chosen not to fund
a distinct category of instruction." Davey was not denied a scholarship
because of who he *was*; he was denied a scholarship because of what he
proposed *to do* — use the funds to prepare for the ministry. Here there is
no question that Trinity Lutheran was denied a grant simply because of
what it is — a church.

The Court in *Locke* also stated that Washington's choice was in keeping
with the State's antiestablishment interest in not using taxpayer funds to
pay for the training of clergy; in fact, the Court could "think of few areas
in which a State's antiestablishment interests come more into play." The
claimant in *Locke* sought funding for an "essentially religious endeavor
. . . akin to a religious calling as well as an academic pursuit," and opposition to such funding "to support church leaders" lay at the historic core
of the Religion Clauses. Here nothing of the sort can be said about a program to use recycled tires to resurface playgrounds.

Relying on *Locke,* the Department nonetheless emphasizes Missouri's similar constitutional tradition of not furnishing taxpayer money directly to churches. But *Locke* took account of Washington's antiestablishment interest only after determining, as noted, that the scholarship program did not "require students to choose between their religious beliefs and receiving a government benefit." As the Court put it, Washington's scholarship program went "a long way toward including religion in its benefits." Students in the program were free to use their scholarships at "pervasively religious schools." Davey could use his scholarship to pursue a secular degree at one institution while studying devotional theology at another. He could also use his scholarship money to attend a religious college and take devotional theology courses there. The only thing he could not do was use the scholarship to pursue a degree in that subject.

In this case, there is no dispute that Trinity Lutheran *is* put to the choice between being a church and receiving a government benefit. The rule is simple: No churches need apply.[2]

C

The State in this case expressly requires Trinity Lutheran to renounce its religious character in order to participate in an otherwise generally available public benefit program, for which it is fully qualified. Our cases make clear that such a condition imposes a penalty on the free exercise of religion that must be subjected to the "most rigorous" scrutiny.

Under that stringent standard, only a state interest "of the highest order" can justify the Department's discriminatory policy. Yet the Department offers nothing more than Missouri's policy preference for skating as far as possible from religious establishment concerns. In the face of the clear infringement on free exercise before us, that interest cannot qualify as compelling. As we said when considering Missouri's same policy preference on a prior occasion, "the state interest asserted here — in achieving greater separation of church and State than is already ensured under the Establishment Clause of the Federal Constitution — is limited by the Free Exercise Clause."

The State has pursued its preferred policy to the point of expressly denying a qualified religious entity a public benefit solely because of

2. This case involves express discrimination based on religious identity with respect to playground resurfacing. We do not address religious uses of funding or other forms of discrimination. [Footnote by the Court]

its religious character. Under our precedents, that goes too far. The Department's policy violates the Free Exercise Clause.[5]

Nearly 200 years ago, a legislator urged the Maryland Assembly to adopt a bill that would end the State's disqualification of Jews from public office: "If, on account of my religious faith, I am subjected to disqualifications, from which others are free, . . . I cannot but consider myself a persecuted man. . . . An odious exclusion from any of the benefits common to the rest of my fellow-citizens, is a persecution, differing only in degree, but of a nature equally unjustifiable with that, whose instruments are chains and torture."

The Missouri Department of Natural Resources has not subjected anyone to chains or torture on account of religion. And the result of the State's policy is nothing so dramatic as the denial of political office. The consequence is, in all likelihood, a few extra scraped knees. But the exclusion of Trinity Lutheran from a public benefit for which it is otherwise qualified, solely because it is a church, is odious to our Constitution all the same, and cannot stand.

Justice THOMAS, with whom Justice GORSUCH joins, concurring in part.

This Court's endorsement in *Locke* of even a "mil[d] kind," *id.,* at 720, 124 S. Ct. 1307 of discrimination against religion remains troubling. But because the Court today appropriately construes *Locke* narrowly, and because no party has asked us to reconsider it, I join nearly all of the Court's opinion. I do not, however, join footnote 3, for the reasons expressed by Justice Gorsuch.

Justice GORSUCH, with whom Justice THOMAS joins, concurring in part.

Missouri's law bars Trinity Lutheran from participating in a public benefits program only because it is a church. I agree this violates the First Amendment and I am pleased to join nearly all of the Court's opinion. I offer only two modest qualifications.

First, the Court leaves open the possibility a useful distinction might be drawn between laws that discriminate on the basis of religious *status* and religious *use.* Respectfully, I harbor doubts about the stability of such a line. Does a religious man say grace before dinner? Or does a man begin his meal in a religious manner? Is it a religious group that built the playground? Or did a group build the playground so it might be used to advance a religious mission? The distinction blurs in much the same way the line between acts and omissions can blur when stared at too long, leaving us to ask (for example) whether the man who drowns by awaiting the incoming tide does so by act (coming upon the sea) or omission (allowing the sea to come upon him). Often enough the same facts can be described both ways.

Neither do I see why the First Amendment's Free Exercise Clause should care. After all, that Clause guarantees the free *exercise* of religion, not just the right to inward belief (or status). And this Court has long explained that government may not "devise mechanisms, overt or disguised, designed to persecute or oppress a religion or its practices." Generally the government may not force people to choose between participation in a public program and their right to free exercise of religion. I don't see why it should matter whether we describe that benefit, say, as closed to Lutherans (status) or closed to people who do Lutheran things (use). It is free exercise either way. For these reasons, reliance on the status-use distinction does not suffice for me to distinguish

Second and for similar reasons, I am unable to join the footnoted observation that "[t]his case involves express discrimination based on religious identity with respect to playground resurfacing." Of course the footnote is entirely correct, but I worry that some might mistakenly read it to suggest that only "playground resurfacing" cases, or only those with some association with children's safety or health, or perhaps some other social good we find sufficiently worthy, are governed by the legal rules recounted in and faithfully applied by the Court's opinion. Such a reading would be unreasonable for our cases are "governed by general principles, rather than ad hoc improvisations." And the general principles here do not permit discrimination against religious exercise—whether on the playground or anywhere else.

Justice BREYER concurring in the judgment.

I agree with much of what the Court says and with its result. But I find relevant, and would emphasize, the particular nature of the "public benefit" here at issue. The Court stated in *Everson* that "cutting off church schools from" such "general government services as ordinary police and fire protection . . . is obviously not the purpose of the Here, the State would cut Trinity Lutheran off from participation in a general program designed to secure or to improve the health and safety of children. I see no significant difference. The fact that the program at issue ultimately funds only a limited number of projects cannot itself justify a religious distinction. Nor is there any administrative or other reason to treat church schools differently. The sole reason advanced that explains the difference is faith. And it is that last-mentioned fact that calls the Free Exercise Clause into play. We need not go further. Public benefits come in many shapes and sizes. I would leave the application of the Free Exercise Clause to other kinds of public benefits for another day.

Justice SOTOMAYOR, with whom Justice GINSBURG joins, dissenting.

To hear the Court tell it, this is a simple case about recycling tires to resurface a playground. The stakes are higher. This case is about nothing less than the relationship between religious institutions and the civil government—that is, between church and state. The Court today profoundly changes that relationship by holding, for the first time, that the Constitution requires the government to provide public funds directly to a church. Its decision slights both our precedents and our history, and its reasoning weakens this country's longstanding commitment to a separation of church and state beneficial to both.

I

Founded in 1922, Trinity Lutheran Church (Church) "operates . . . for the express purpose of carrying out the commission of . . . Jesus Christ as directed to His church on earth." The Church uses "preaching, teaching, worship, witness, service, and fellowship according to the Word of God" to carry out its mission "to 'make disciples.'" The Church's religious beliefs include its desire to "associat[e] with the [Trinity Church Child] Learning Center." The Learning Center serves as "a ministry of the Church and incorporates daily religion and developmentally appropriate activities into . . . [its] program." In this way, "[t]hrough the Learning Center, the Church teaches a Christian world view to children of members of the Church, as well as children of non-member residents" of the area. These activities represent the Church's "sincere religious belief . . . to use [the Learning Center] to teach the Gospel to children of its members, as well to bring the Gospel message to non-members."

II

Properly understood then, this is a case about whether Missouri can decline to fund improvements to the facilities the Church uses to practice and spread its religious views. This Court has repeatedly warned that funding of exactly this kind—payments from the government to a house of worship—would cross the line drawn by the Establishment Clause. So it is surprising that the Court mentions the Establishment Clause only to note the parties' agreement that it "does not prevent Missouri from including Trinity Lutheran in the Scrap Tire Program." Constitutional questions are decided by this Court, not the parties' concessions. The Establishment Clause does not allow Missouri to grant the Church's funding request because the Church uses the Learning Center, including its playground, in conjunction with its religious mission. The Court's silence on this front signals either its misunderstanding of the facts of this case or a startling departure from our precedents.

The government may not directly fund religious exercise. Nowhere is this rule more clearly implicated than when funds flow directly from the public treasury to a house of worship. A house of worship exists to foster and further religious exercise. When a government funds a house of worship, it underwrites this religious exercise.

This case is no different. The Church seeks state funds to improve the Learning Center's facilities, which, by the Church's own avowed description, are used to assist the spiritual growth of the children of its members and to spread the Church's faith to the children of nonmembers. The Church's playground surface — like a Sunday School room's walls or the sanctuary's pews — are integrated with and integral to its religious mission. The conclusion that the funding the Church seeks would impermissibly advance religion is inescapable.

True, this Court has found some direct government funding of religious institutions to be consistent with the Establishment Clause. But the funding in those cases came with assurances that public funds would not be used for religious activity, despite the religious nature of the institution. The Church has not and cannot provide such assurances here. The Church has a religious mission, one that it pursues through the Learning Center. The playground surface cannot be confined to secular use any more than lumber used to frame the Church's walls, glass stained and used to form its windows, or nails used to build its altar.

The Court may simply disagree with this account of the facts and think that the Church does not put its playground to religious use. If so, its mistake is limited to this case. But if it agrees that the State's funding would further religious activity and sees no Establishment Clause problem, then it must be implicitly applying a rule other than the one agreed to in our precedents.

When the Court last addressed direct funding of religious institutions, in *Mitchell,* it adhered to the rule that the Establishment Clause prohibits the direct funding of religious activities.

Today's opinion suggests the Court has made the leap the *Mitchell* plurality could not. For if it agrees that the funding here will finance religious activities, then only a rule that considers that fact irrelevant could support a conclusion of constitutionality. It has no basis in the history to which the Court has repeatedly turned to inform its understanding of the

Establishment Clause. It permits direct subsidies for religious indoctrination, with all the attendant concerns that led to the Establishment Clause. And it favors certain religious groups, those with a belief system that allows them to compete for public dollars and those well-organized and well-funded enough to do so successfully.

Such a break with precedent would mark a radical mistake. The Establishment Clause protects both religion and government from the dangers that result when the two become entwined, "*not* by providing every religion with an *equal opportunity* (say, to secure state funding or to pray in the public schools), but by drawing fairly clear lines of *separation* between church and state—at least where the heartland of religious belief, such as primary religious [worship], is at issue."

## III

Even assuming the absence of an Establishment Clause violation and proceeding on the Court's preferred front—the Free Exercise Clause—the Court errs. It claims that the government may not draw lines based on an entity's religious "status." But we have repeatedly said that it can. When confronted with government action that draws such a line, we have carefully considered whether the interests embodied in the Religion Clauses justify that line. The question here is thus whether those interests support the line drawn in Missouri's Article I, § 7, separating the State's treasury from those of houses of worship. They unquestionably do.

The Establishment Clause prohibits laws "respecting an establishment of religion" and the Free Exercise Clause prohibits laws "prohibiting the free exercise thereof." "[I]f expanded to a logical extreme," these prohibitions "would tend to clash with the other." Even in the absence of a violation of one of the Religion Clauses, the interaction of government and religion can raise concerns that sound in both Clauses. For that reason, the government may sometimes act to accommodate those concerns, even when not required to do so by the Free Exercise Clause, without violating the Establishment Clause. And the government may sometimes act to accommodate those concerns, even when not required to do so by the Establishment Clause, without violating the Free Exercise Clause. "[T]here is room for play in the joints productive of a benevolent neutrality which will permit religious exercise to exist without sponsorship and without interference." This space between the two Clauses gives government some room to recognize the unique status of religious entities and to single them out on that basis for exclusion from otherwise generally applicable laws.

Invoking this principle, this Court has held that the government may sometimes relieve religious entities from the requirements of government programs. A State need not, for example, require nonprofit houses of worship to pay property taxes. Nor must a State require nonprofit religious entities to abstain from making employment decisions on the basis of religion. But the government may not invoke the space between the Religion Clauses in a manner that "devolve[s] into an unlawful fostering of religion."

Missouri has decided that the unique status of houses of worship requires a special rule when it comes to public funds. Its Constitution reflects that choice and provides:

"That no money shall ever be taken from the public treasury, directly or indirectly, in aid of any church, sect, or denomination of religion, or in aid of any priest, preacher, minister or teacher thereof, as such; and that no preference shall be given to nor any discrimination made against any church, sect or creed of religion, or any form of religious faith or worship." Art. I, § 7.

Missouri's decision, which has deep roots in our Nation's history, reflects a reasonable and constitutional judgment.

This Court has consistently looked to history for guidance when applying the Constitution's Religion Clauses. Those Clauses guard against a return to the past, and so that past properly informs their meaning. This case is no different.

Those who fought to end the public funding of religion based their opposition on a powerful set of arguments, all stemming from the basic premise that the practice harmed both civil government and religion. The civil government, they maintained, could claim no authority over religious belief. For them, support for religion compelled by the State marked an overstep of authority that would only lead to more. Equally troubling, it risked divisiveness by giving religions reason to compete for the State's beneficence. Faith, they believed, was a personal matter, entirely between an individual and his god. Religion was best served when sects reached out on the basis of their tenets alone, unsullied by outside forces, allowing adherents to come to their faith voluntarily. Over and over, these arguments gained acceptance and led to the end of state laws exacting payment for the support of religion.

In *Locke,* this Court expressed an understanding of, and respect for, this history.

The same is true of this case, about directing taxpayer funds to houses of worship. Like the use of public dollars for ministers at issue in *Locke,* turning over public funds to houses of worship implicates serious antiestablishment and free exercise interests. The history just discussed fully supports this conclusion. As states disestablished, they repealed laws allowing taxation to support religion because the practice threatened other forms of government support for, involved some government control over, and weakened supporters' control of religion. Common sense also supports this conclusion. Recall that a state may not fund religious activities without violating the Establishment Clause. A state can reasonably use status as a "house of worship" as a stand-in for "religious activities." Inside a house of worship, dividing the religious from the secular would require intrusive line-drawing by government, and monitoring those lines would entangle government with the house of worship's activities. And so while not every activity a house of worship undertakes will be inseparably linked to religious activity, "the likelihood that many are makes a categorical rule a suitable means to avoid chilling the exercise of religion." Finally, and of course, such funding implicates the free exercise rights of taxpayers by denying them the chance to decide for themselves whether and how to fund religion. If there is any " 'room for play in the joints' between" the Religion Clauses, it is here.

As was true in *Locke,* a prophylactic rule against the use of public funds for houses of worship is a permissible accommodation of these weighty interests. The rule has a historical pedigree identical to that of the provision in Today, thirty-eight States have a counterpart to Missouri's Article I, § 7. The provisions, as a general matter, date back to or before these States' original Constitutions. That so many States have for so long drawn a line that prohibits public funding for houses of worship, based on principles rooted in this Nation's understanding of how best to foster religious liberty, supports the conclusion that public funding of houses of worship "is of a different ilk."

Missouri has recognized the simple truth that, even absent an Establishment Clause violation, the transfer of public funds to houses of worship raises concerns that sit exactly between the Religion Clauses. To avoid those concerns, and only those concerns, it has prohibited such funding. In doing so, it made the same choice made by the earliest States centuries ago and many other States in the years since. The Constitution permits this choice.

In the Court's view, none of this matters. It focuses on one aspect of Missouri's Article I, § 7, to the exclusion of all else: that it denies funding to a house of worship, here the Church, "simply because of what it [i]s — a church."

Start where the Court stays silent. Its opinion does not acknowledge that our precedents have expressly approved of a government's choice to draw lines based on an entity's religious status. Those cases did not deploy strict scrutiny to create a presumption of unconstitutionality, as the Court does today. Instead, they asked whether the government had offered a strong enough reason to justify drawing a line based on that status.

The Court takes two steps to avoid these precedents. First, it recasts *Locke* as a case about a restriction that prohibited the would-be minister from "us[ing] the funds to prepare for the ministry." A faithful reading of *Locke* gives it a broader reach. *Locke* stands for the reasonable proposition that the government may, but need not, choose not to fund certain religious entities (there, ministers) where doing so raises "historic and substantial" establishment and free exercise concerns.

Second, it suggests that this case is different because it involves "discrimination" in the form of the denial of access to a possible benefit. But in this area of law, a decision to treat entities differently based on distinctions that the Religion Clauses make relevant does not amount to discrimination. To understand why, keep in mind that "the Court has unambiguously concluded that the individual freedom of conscience protected by the First Amendment embraces the right to select any religious faith or none at all." If the denial of a benefit others may receive is discrimination that violates the Free Exercise Clause, then the accommodations of religious entities we have approved would violate the free exercise rights of nonreligious entities. We have, with good reason, rejected that idea and instead focused on whether the government has provided a good enough reason, based in the values the Religion Clauses protect, for its decision.

The Court offers no real reason for rejecting the balancing approach in our precedents in favor of strict scrutiny, beyond its references to discrimination. The Court's desire to avoid what it views as discrimination is understandable. But in this context, the description is particularly inappropriate. A State's decision not to fund houses of worship does not disfavor religion; rather, it represents a valid choice to remain secular in the face of serious establishment and free exercise concerns. That does not make the State "atheistic or antireligious." The Court's conclusion "that the only alternative to governmental support of religion is governmental hostility to it represents a giant step backward in our Religion Clause jurisprudence."

At bottom, the Court creates the following rule today: The government may draw lines on the basis of religious status to grant a benefit to religious persons or entities but it may not draw lines on that basis when doing so would further the interests the Religion Clauses protect in other ways. Nothing supports this lopsided outcome. Not the Religion Clauses, as they protect establishment and free exercise interests in the same constitutional breath, neither privileged over the other. Not precedent, since we have repeatedly explained that the Clauses protect not religion but "the individual's freedom of conscience," — that which allows him to choose religion, reject it, or remain undecided. And not reason, because as this case shows, the same interests served by lifting government-imposed burdens on certain religious entities may sometimes be equally served by denying government-provided benefits to certain religious entities.[3] Today's decision discounts centuries of history and jeopardizes the government's ability to remain secular.

## IV

The Court today dismantles a core protection for religious freedom provided in these Clauses. It holds not just that a government may support houses of worship with taxpayer funds, but that — at least in this case and perhaps in others, it must do so whenever it decides to create a funding program. History shows that the Religion Clauses separate the public treasury from religious coffers as one measure to secure the kind of freedom of conscience that benefits both religion and government. If this separation means anything, it means that the government cannot, or at the very least need not, tax its citizens and turn that money over to houses of worship. The Court today blinds itself to the outcome this history requires and leads us instead to a place where separation of church and state is a constitutional slogan, not a constitutional commitment.

---

3. In the end, the soundness of today's decision may matter less than what it might enable tomorrow. The principle it establishes can be manipulated to call for a similar fate for lines drawn on the basis of religious use. It is enough for today to explain why the Court's decision is wrong. The error of the concurrences' hoped-for decisions can be left for tomorrow. [Footnote by Justice SOTOMAYOR]